MINISTRY *Chick*

Find Your Community,
Own Your Leadership,
Take Your Step!

MELISSA MASHBURN

Published by Market Refined Publishing,
An Imprint of Market Refined Media, LLC
193 Cleo Circle
Ringgold GA 30736
marketrefinedmedia.com

Cover and Interior Design by Nelly Murariu at PixBeeDesigns.com
Manuscript Edits by Carolyn Reed Master and Market Refined Media

Print ISBN: 979-8-9855797-9-6
Digital ISBN: 979-8-9868023-0-5

Library of Congress Control Number: 2022915399

First Edition: September 2022

Contents

Preface

Hello, Friend,

If you picked up this book, then I am hoping you realize you are not alone in your journey as a female leader in the ministry. I'm also praying that by the time you finish this adventure with me you will realize that you are more than just . . . whatever you used to want to say next about yourself. But more than anything, it's my prayer that you are picking up this book because you are a female leader in the ministry, and you are ready to move beyond the titles, hats, and other things that are put on you by your boss and even others in the ministry, so you can be the very best leader you can be as you faithfully serve.

I get it, though, because I've been labeled a pastor's wife, pastor, ministry leader, ministry director, super volunteer, and so many other strange and ambiguous things in between. Yet, whatever your role is at the church, you are way more than what you do in the ministry. Over the last twenty years I've served in the local church in just about every role except for student ministry. That was only out of respect for my own kids at the time, because my husband Matt and I really felt like they needed their own place to be that their parents were not immediately involved in or leading.

It's my goal throughout the course of this book to walk alongside you as you find your community, own your leadership, and take your next step to wherever God might be leading you. I know, boy do I know, that it can be and might be scary, but if there is one thing that I know now more than ever it's this . . . the Church needs you. We need your gifts, your skills, your leadership, and your voice in the ministry now more than ever. With over 60% of those attending our churches being women, they need to see strong, confident, Jesus-loving women in the ministry who are using their gifts for the Kingdom. They need to see it and so does the next generation of women in the Church.

We need strong female leaders that have walked the road and can share their journey with others. I wish I had this information in my hands when I first started out in ministry. I was so passionate and on fire for God and willing to do whatever it takes for the local church. I had fire in my belly, but it was an all-consuming fire at times that accidentally burned a few people, even myself.

We need that passion and excitement, but we also need well trained, thoughtful, solid female leaders who are grounded in their faith and in their identity. This is not cockiness, but a holy confidence balanced with humility that is in the ready position for whatever God has in store next. This kind of self-awareness and readiness doesn't happen overnight, it happens over time with intentional and deliberate learning, training, and understanding. It takes hard work to get deep down in our hearts to make sure they are pure, clean, and focused wholly on God and His will.

When the motive of our heart is out of alignment with God's design, timing, or intent, we can put our own personal agenda on the center stage of our ministry efforts. There is no room for self-promotion and manipulation in this role. Oh, I've been there, and unfortunately even done that for a season, and here's what it gets you—burned out, worn out, exhausted, and unfulfilled. There can be a seductive lure of celebrity that is flashy and can feel like you've made it, but do not be deceived, God deserves all the honor and glory and if you start to focus on you, more than you do Him, then you are headed for a heap of trouble.

We're going to walk through a lot of stories and real-life ministry experiences together in this book and it's my prayer that at the end of our time together you will realize that you are more than just the title you have or the role you fulfill; you are a beautiful, wonderful child of God and He has uniquely prepared you to serve Him in mighty ways. But that service must be out of an overflow of your love for Him, not the first and foremost thing that you do or even who you are.

You are more than that.

You are His and He has called you to this season of your life and ministry.

It's a high calling and a great adventure, truly one that is better when He leads, and you have a few trusted friends to go on the journey with you. I pray that you find that camaraderie here within these pages and can't wait to hear all about what He is doing in and through you because of it.

Foreword *by Kadi Cole*

She was standing in the back of the conference room lingering but not getting in line, keeping loose eye contact but trying not to be attention-grabbing, pleasantly smiling but keeping a little quiet. I didn't know this woman, yet I knew I was just like her.

Maybe you're also a woman whose faith keeps you centered but who's leadership gifts are calling you to more? You can make an entrance, but rarely do. You have something to say, but often defer to others. You long to make a difference but aren't sure how. If you ever find yourself caught between being not enough and yet too much, then you are one of us . . . those with potential, those who hunger, those who are trying yet aren't ever *really* sure of ourselves and our leadership.

It only took 30 seconds for my suspicions to be confirmed about Melissa . . . she's hardly a stand-in-the-background kind of gal. When the line in front of me finally subsided, she slowly made her way forward and introduced herself. *Of course . . . you're Melissa!* We had already met online because she is that kind of leader—warm, connected, energetic, engaging, and caring. We had built a loose connection through the Ministry Chick Facebook Group (which you should absolutely join right now. It's okay, stop and take a minute to sign up. We'll wait.) And now God was doing something new in and for both of us. I could *feel* it.

That's what Melissa does. She connects with people, bringing all her joy and wisdom and seasoned leadership, and then she helps build something new. I was a new author at the time, with a surprise best seller trying to say yes to the opportunities coming at me that put me in front of large groups of male pastors and leaders. And at the same time, I was equally longing to help female church leaders know they are not alone, get the encouragement they are often missing, and accelerate their ability to build a professional network of their own to equip them in their calling. It was no small task, and I was feeling under-equipped and overwhelmed. Then God sent Melissa. She stepped into Ministry Chick to bring leadership, relationship, and a good dose of fun. She transformed our fledgling social media group into a tribe of nearly three thousand female ministry leaders who are constantly helping and supporting each other as we all answer the call of God in our lives.

What new thing is God calling you to? I know He has something, and I also know you aren't meant to build it alone. The great news is that God has also brought you exactly the right people. Melissa and the team of contributors to this book will both uplift your heart and blow your mind. Get ready. It's time to find your community, own your leadership, and take your next step. You can do it.

And I'll be cheering you on the entire way!

Kadi

Kadi Cole
Author of *Developing Female Leaders* and *Find Your Leadership Voice in 90 Days*
Founder of Ministry Chick and Kadi Cole & Company
www.kadicole.com
@kadicole

Introduction:
Welcome to Ministry Chick!

Welcome to ministry. Whether you are new to ministry or have been walking this road for a while, I am so glad you are joining the conversation. We need you to be the best possible version of yourself (as a leader and as a woman), and it is my prayer that this book will give you the tips, tricks, and tools you will need to do so.

Just to give you a little insight, this is probably the last thing I ever thought I would write. I literally sat down to write a book on the importance of godly friendships in your life, but after I started writing these words just started to pour out from my heart onto the pages. The hard part about that is if you knew me, really knew me, you would know that I wrestle with one big gaping messy question pretty much all the time and that question is, "Who do you think you are?" It's a question that has literally plagued me since the fourth grade. I don't think my teacher, whom I will not name publicly, meant any harm by her statement. But at the time, on a young impressionable heart, it negatively grafted itself deep down into my soul causing me to question myself daily.

In the years that followed, it unofficially became the question that came up pretty much any time I tried to go for a dream or big project. It needled me, poked at me, and caused me to doubt myself, my abilities, those who loved me, and everything in between. This uncertainty and lack of confidence really held me captive for too many years. It took years of experience, maturity, and solid biblical Christian counseling to get to the other side of that question. I can see now that this one single question was the driver behind some of my perfectionism, workaholism, and years of feeling less than—one single question from what a fourth-grade teacher said as a reprimand to an overachieving, overactive, and excited young girl.

The hard part of this overarching theme of trying to earn everyone's approval, which was this great big revelation in my life, was that it came upon me in the middle of over a decade of ministry. It came crashing in on me while I had worked at two thriving churches that were at the time growing and looked good on the outside and yet they were also deeply unhealthy internally. As a growing church that was wrestling with the demands of the growth, the busyness and unrealistic expectations started to catch up to not only my heart but my body as well. I didn't know it and did not even appreciate what was going on inside or around me, but it became a driver to push myself more, and work harder to be . . . well . . . the best. I was going to be the hardest working, the most informed, have the greatest number of volunteers, you name it. I wanted to be (and wanted the ministries that I led to be) the example for others. Yeah, I know, you hear the downfall coming, don't you? The ugly part is that all of that was based off *me* and *my* gifts, and *my* skills, and *my* abilities. You heard me correctly, I was neck deep in the ministry and yet relying on myself and my skills and not leaning on God. I don't say this lightly, nor is it something that I am proud of, but it is my hope that maybe this helps you along the way as you lead in the ministry.

This book in your hands is twenty years in the making. It's everything I wish I had known when I first started out in ministry as well as everything, I wish I had known about who God is, who He created me to be, and how we can and should work together and lean on each other to accomplish His will on earth. My story is one full of lessons learned the hard way and it's my hope that in by sharing some of what I have learned along the way that you will be able to short cut, skip over, or even shorten the learning curve for you because, my friend, there is a learning curve to this thing called life, especially life in the ministry as a female leader.

I know that this book will not be exhaustive and cover everything you have questions about, but it's my hope that it will cover some of the major themes that you might encounter as a female leader in ministry. It's the culmination of decades of work with women as a ministry leader, pastor, friend, coach, mentor and everything in between. I hope by the end of our time together you walk away with this—a clear understanding of who you are in Christ and how you can find your community, own your leadership, and take your next step.

Whatever that step might be, I know there might be a little voice inside of your head (like there was in mine) that is right now saying, "Who do you think you are?" We are going to squash that question with the truth of who God says you are by digging into Scripture, seeking wisdom (James 1:5) allowing His Word to define our identity and not leaning on our understanding (Proverbs 3:5) but fully leaning into who He says you are as His daughter and His leader in the Church—His voice to a lost and lonely world.

Who does He say you are, my friend?

You are loved (1 John 4:10-12),

You are His (Deuteronomy 7:6),

You have gifts and skills (1 Corinthians 12:1-11),

He needs and wants you to use them for the body of Christ (1 Corinthians 12:7),

He will not leave you (John 14:16),

He will not forsake you (Hebrews 13:5),

He has called you (Ephesians 1:18),

He has given you a spirit of power, love, and self-discipline (2 Timothy 1:7),

He has qualified you (2 Corinthians 3:4-6),

He has equipped you (2 Timothy 3:17),

He has prepared you (Romans 9:23),

You are ready to get to work, because you are more than just . . . the labels that others put on you or you even put on yourself.

Here's how I know this—I've lived it and carried it around for most of my life, burdened by the weight of everyone else's expectations of me and for me. Yes, even as a Christ follower, and yes, even as a female leader in the ministry. The reality is that we are human. When Christ enters our hearts, our eternities are changed, but we still have work to do on our "stuff". Thankfully through lots of growth, counseling, prayer, and learning things the hard way by the grace of God I can see just how heavy that "not enough" burden has been on me as well as my ministry.

God can and does use anyone He chooses to do His work. He takes broken-down, every-day, ordinary people to do His extraordinary work, and it is truly magnificent to see.

Once we let go of everyone else's expectations and labels, we can truly rest in the label He has given us as His child(ren). "But to all who did receive him, who believed in his name, he gave the right to become children of God" (John 1:12, ESV).

It's been a painful and bumpy journey at times, *but God* (I love those two words together, don't you?) has done something miraculous in me that I hope to share with you so that you can find your community, own your leadership, and take your next step to wherever He is leading you— even right now as you read this!

Who do you think you are?

I'm so glad you asked . . . I am His and I am here to do His work.

Let's get this party started, shall we?

Section One

YOU ARE MORE THAN JUST _____

What I Wish I Knew
When I Started in the Ministry
as a Female Leader

Chapter 1

YOU ARE MORE THAN JUST:
THE TITLE YOU HAVE

When I sit with female leaders, the first question that typically comes up is, "What do you do?" We've become so accustomed to identifying ourselves with what we do. What we do is a job; it's not who we are. It's a part of us, but it isn't us. At least not completely. The same is true with your specific title in the ministry. Let's face it. Every church has a very different position on what roles and titles women are permitted to have according to their denomination's theology on gender. Some churches are complementarian, and some are egalitarian, while others are a messy mix of both. Regardless, many of us female leaders may not ever get certain titles like leader, shepherd, pastor, or minister. It doesn't mean you aren't those things; it simply means your church doesn't acknowledge women holding those roles as titles.

I remember starting in my second ministry position. It was one of my favorites, but when I was interviewing for the position, the pastor gently mentioned to me that they do not believe that women can or should be called or have the title of "pastor". Well, that was very unexpected. It was something that I had worked hard for at my previous church, and it took years of hard work to be licensed in a ceremony in front of my peers as a pastor at that church (in the same denomination as the one that I was moving to at the second church, by the way). I sat there feeling a little bewildered and shocked. This title was something that was a part of me, part of my calling, and part of what God had done in my life, but now this pastor said I had to give it up and be a "director" instead. Which, okay, isn't the end of the world, but it was a hard pill to swallow at the time, because, after all, I had worked hard to earn that title, and this felt like a step back in some ways—even if it was mostly a shot to my ego. It just didn't seem fair to me at that time. After a lot of prayer and discussion with my husband, friends, and even mentors, I decided that I could lay down that "title" because that's what it was—a manmade title. I knew that I was still called to pastor/shepherd people, so I could and would do so without the title before my name.

Honestly, as hard as it was to process in the beginning, I was soon able to lay it down and be okay with it. In the meantime, God had started to really work on my heart and helped me see that my identity is not in the title that others give me, but my identity is in *Him* and the title *He* gives me. It was not an easy—nor was it a quick—process, but I can see now (got to love 20/20 hindsight) that I had become so consumed with the title that it was holding me back from just being me—Melissa.

What about you? Is there a title that you have that has become a badge of honor that you wear? I'm not saying that you don't deserve the praise, the accolades, or even the power of that title, but is it becoming an idol?

That's where the heart work comes in. Your title is child of God, not pastor, director, coordinator, associate, assistant, or what other title you have in your role as a female leader. What if, no matter what the title is, we simply worked as if it really didn't matter?

"Whatever you do, work heartily, as for the Lord and not for men." (Colossians 3:23, ESV)

If we are leaders—and I am guessing that if you are reading this book, then you are a leader—the reality is that we all have influence; it's just a matter of what we are doing with it and whether we are being intentional about it. What if we poured out our heart and soul in every project simply because we've been given an opportunity to make a difference for the kingdom?

How do you even begin to do that? Great question! And I hear you. I get it. I literally worked my entire ministry career for this pinnacle moment only to have it taken away. Okay, so I willingly laid it down, but at the time it felt like it was taken away.

Therefore, it is so incredibly important that before you move on to anything else I have to share, that you make sure you are firmly rooted in your identity in Christ. I know you might think you are solid here but take it from someone that has been around this block a few times, there are a lot of strong leaders in the ministry world who struggle with their identity in Christ. The world and all its trappings: notoriety, money, stuff, climbing the ladder in the organization, looking and living a "Pinterest perfect" life are all very tempting. They can lure the best of us to be focused on the "things of this world" and not even realize that we have drifted a little off course.

I think it's also a good time to take a moment to pause and discuss the whole idea of a job and a calling. Some of you might work at a job. You go in, work hard, do your best, and go home. You are a child of God, so of course you want to work as if working for the Lord, but your job may be completely different from your calling.

Practically speaking, a job is what you are paid to do and accomplish for your organization. Anyone can get a job. That is the nature of the world we live in. A calling, on the other hand, is something that God has given to you specifically as the purpose and passion of your life. A calling is what will carry you through when the demands of the "job" get to be too much at times. The calling God gives you is unique to you. It is the thing that you would do even if you did not get paid for it. It drives you. You live it, breathe it, think about it, pray about it, and have those "this is what I was made for" mountain top moments in fulfillment of a calling. You can be excited and feel proud of your work at a job, but it still might feel like it is missing something if your job doesn't engage your calling.

You can also have a job in which God has specifically called you to serve the people or the mission there. Okay, that may sound a little confusing, but here's the thing that I hope makes sense in its most basic form—God can and will use you wherever you are if you are willing to be used by Him—whether it is in your dream job, a regular "provides the paycheck" job, or working in the ministry.

For example, you might be employed at your church doing payroll, but you know that's not your calling (it can be, but for the sake of this example we will say it's not). Your calling is in hospitality and making sure people feel welcome. Because your job doesn't satisfy your calling, you may serve on the First Impressions team at your church on the weekend or by hosting a group of new believers in your home once a month.

What you do is not who you are; it is an expression of who you are. It's a part of you, but it does not define you. Your job is an element of your gifts that God uses of you in this world but if we are not careful, we can easily become distracted and so focused on getting the perfect job "at the church" that we can easily forget that we can all live out our calling every day—no matter what job or job title we have. And better yet, we can live it out even if we don't have the title we desire or deserve.

I've heard people say, "I am not a leader because I don't even have a title", or "I am just a volunteer in the ministry" a lot lately. I would caution you from jumping into that "less than" mentality because you don't have a particular title or because you are a volunteer. We are all called to serve the Kingdom and your role might look different than mine, but that does not make it any more or less important. We each have work to do, and we need every single one of us working to do what He has called us to do while we are here (1 Corinthians 12).

Chances are that you are doing way more than you even think. Don't minimize it because you think you needs a title, a paycheck, or a leader to notice you to validate your unique service.

Real Ministry Chick Experience
from Crystal Stine

Colossians 3:23 in the Message says, "Do your best. Work from the heart for your real Master, for God, confident that you'll get paid in full when you come into your inheritance. Keep in mind always that the ultimate Master you're serving is Christ." That verse is one that changed my heart and challenged my idea of what it meant to be successful.

While other girls were dreaming of their weddings or their future husbands or the number of kids they would have, I was dreaming of my career. I desperately wanted an answer to "What do you want to do when you grow up?" and along the way I lost sight of the fact that I should have been trying to answer a better question: "Who do You want to be when you grow up, God?" My identity was firmly rooted in my role, my title, my contributions, and my successes, so when I experienced failures and detours, my identity was shaken.

If I'm fully transparent, I'm really, really good at working. I love to work. Using my gifts and passions to serve an organization brings me joy. But for years I spent my time striving after the next promotion or opportunity for recognition—I was working the way the world expected, and instead of feeling fulfilled and accomplished, I was weary, frustrated, and empty. Something was missing because even when my jobs changed and I began working in ministry, I still felt lost.

That was the beginning of a journey with the Lord that led me to write books like *Holy Hustle* and *Quieting the Shout of Should*. As I unpacked privately what God was revealing—that my identity wasn't in Christ, that success and busyness had become idols, and that I lacked the humility to receive what He had next for me—He asked me to share parts of the journey publicly.

When we set aside our pride and commit to working well for the Lord, we can stop striving for fancy titles that tell the world we're worthy. God has already chosen you, to use your gifts and talents for His kingdom, right where you are. Your mission field is the field you stand in today, and you can shine the spotlight on God and proclaim the Gospel at home, in the grocery store, in the school drop-offline, on social media, or in a formal ministry role, to an audience of one or thousands.

The number of hats you wear, the titles you hold, nor the extra work you desperately wish someone would acknowledge, will ever make you more valuable to the Lord. You are His, and He loves you. In Christ we find our true identity as beloved children of God. Work hard, rest well, and serve the Lord with confidence.

When I coach female leaders, one of the first things we talk about are core values. Why? Because you must have a firm idea of what's important to you to be able to filter through all the other things that are not as important. These core values will allow you to figure out if something is just "off" or doesn't feel right. They can help you as you have opportunities to come your way to see if they are in alignment with who you are and what is important to you. They can be guardrails in your ministry that serve as protective barriers to keep you safe, healthy, and on track in what your stated goals are, and the unique and specific purpose God has for your life.

"When your values are clear to you,
making decisions becomes easier." – Roy Disney[1]

So why is it important to know what our core values are? It's important because if you can't identify them, you will constantly be blown around by other people's opinions and values. When that happens there is a disconnect and a feeling deep down inside of us that something isn't right. We might not even be able to pinpoint directly why it isn't right, but we do know it rubs us the wrong way or maybe even grates on our nerves. Have you ever spent some time around someone and something about them just doesn't sit right with you? You can't always pinpoint what "it" is, but when you are in touch with your values, you can be sure that it's probably bumping up against your core values, which can cause an adverse reaction in your connection to them.

Here's an example of what I am talking about: imagine having a ministry friend whose whole platform was based on living authentically, only to notice how very often she posts selfies or a filtered view of her life. That would seem contradictory and would call the credibility of her value on the message of being "real" into question. Now imagine if you have a personal core value about authenticity! Hello! This person would be hard to follow or engage with because she not only violates her own stated value with implications of the contrary, but she rubs against your own core value.

It's up to you to guide the choices you make to define your values, but please remember that these are unique to you. Other people won't necessarily share your core values. This is why it is so important to determine the choices you make to define and defend your values. They are just as unique to you as the ministry God has given you.

The hard part is when you live outside of what you value, going where He didn't send you, working, living, and doing things that just do not line up with who Christ created you to be. When this happens, you can experience increased stress, anxiety, discontentment, and the blurring of boundaries you need in your life to keep you going where God is leading you. Everything you do in your life is about choices and they are made based on what you value. What we value is usually a reflection of what is truly important to us, so making sure you know what you value can help you to live a truly purposeful life. It also helps you filter through any jobs, opportunities, projects, or even people that come into your life. When you decide ahead of time what your core values are then you can be intentional about living your life and ministry the way God specifically created you.

When I sat with Kadi Cole, my mentor and coach, to work through what my core values were, I found there were three specific sections of those values: Some represent *my authentic self*, some crossed over to how I interact with *people*, and the last few focused on *who I choose to be*. While this break down might not be the case for everyone, I have found that it is a good idea to dig in and find out what your core values are. Here's some questions to answer to get started on discovering yours:

» When you were a child (early elementary school age), what were 6-7 qualities that described you?

» What are some things that you are passionate about doing?

» Think of a time during the last 15 years when you felt you were living your best self. What are a few characteristic traits of yourself at that time?

» If you were to write down a list of the top 10 values that people would need to have a successful life, what would you list?

Now, go back through all the above questions and think about what your top five values might be based on each of the responses. These are most likely your top five values.

Your core values can serve as a thermometer to gauge your inner health. If you are unhealthy, it will show up in your everyday life. I'm not talking about your height, weight, or anything outward; I'm talking about the things deep down in your heart (Proverbs 4:23). I know this because I went through it. I did not even realize how unhealthy I was until I was on the edge of burnout. You see, I never dug into my core values, nor my identity in Christ, when I first started leading in the ministry. I was fresh, young, inexperienced, and super passionate about making a difference in the local church. I was a sinner saved by grace as an adult and I knew how much He had radically changed my life. I was confident that God could and would use me.

What I didn't realize was that, yes, while I was a new creation (2 Corinthians 5:17) and He had washed me clean (Psalm 51:7), I was still the old me in a lot of ways. This means I still carried junk with me even in my new role. I was working "for" the Church and in many ways that can exacerbate any underlying things we still need to work on.

For me, it turned into perfectionism and workaholism. The demands of ministry pushed on my "not good enough" buttons in ways that I wasn't fully prepared to deal with, so I became driven to an unhealthy level. It wasn't until a few years later that I even noticed it. Yes, people did try to point it out, but my immaturity in the faith and my lack of awareness of my core values allowed me to be swallowed up by the demands of ministry. This is why it is so incredibly important to know that you are more than the title you have or role you serve in this season of your life and leadership.

Understanding your core values along with having a strong identity in Christ will set you up for a long, healthy, productive season of ministry. We do not need here today, gone tomorrow women in ministry. We need female leaders that are here for the long haul, who live, breathe, and serve from a heart that loves God and wants to serve Him here on earth. We need that from you! Please do the heart work now so that you can be strong, confident, and ready to go wherever He sends you.

Real Ministry Chick Experience

from Jessie Cruickshank

These days I think of identity and calling as two sides of the same coin. I like to think that my calling flows out of my identity in Christ. I may have talents and skills, but they should not exist apart from or outside of the space of redemption in my identity in Christ. When we are young, our identity is informed, in part, by our community. I always wanted to be teachable, and I think I leaned too much into other people's opinion and perception of me to help shape that identity—especially my identity and calling as a leader. I embraced any formative instruction they gave me, but eventually I started to feel lost and tossed about by the whims of others' agenda for my development.

Upon reflection, I realized that nobody had asked me who I thought I was created to be. They all had their own opinions of what my calling was. Nobody asked me what God was saying to me about it. I had become a chameleon rather than a leader with competencies and boundaries. I needed to get all the other voices and opinions out of my head so I could learn to hear my own voice. I needed a solid starting point of 'me' rather than always modifying and adapting it. This led to the advent of a season of being 'unteachable,' trusting God to later refine and shape what I discovered about myself.

It was a three-year journey learning to be comfortable in my own skin. I learned to be comfortable with my own voice, my own heart, my own hands (skills), and my own two feet (experience). It wasn't easy. It was hard to learn how much of my calling and identity formation I had outsourced to other people and their opinions or agendas. The good news is that I have indeed learned to be comfortable in my own skin, with my own voice, heart, hands, and feet. I believe my leadership flows out from my identity in Christ, and the more those have come into alignment, the greater my impact has been, regardless of position or title.

I've invited some of my friends from the Facebook group called Ministry Chick to share some of their thoughts on this topic, and when you see it in the book it will be listed as Chick Chat. If you would like more information about the Ministry Chick Facebook community, please go to the back of the book for more info on connecting with us. I know you will be blessed and encouraged by their ideas.

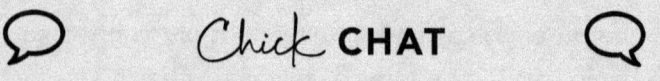

Chick **CHAT**

Real, practical advice on being a female leader in the ministry and struggling to not let your title or role at the church define you as a person.

> Be "all there," wherever you are. Doing your best at work and at home happens when you are fully present to God, yourself, and those around you.
> – Rosemarie

> Define God's purpose for your life by writing a purpose statement supported by a biblical reference. Then

keep it posted on your phone screen to be reminded regularly that the reason you do what you do is because of who God made you to be. – Jerra

I wrote on my mirror who I am statements . . . I am a child of God, I am called by God, I am a . . . so I can remind myself daily I am more than my ministry role.
 – Sara

Keep the Sabbath—make it a priority that is more important than any task my job requires. When I honor the Sabbath, I'm able to do to more, I have a clear mind, and my week never feels overwhelming or unmanageable. I also have hobbies and friends outside of the Church. It's also important for me to have a wide variety of information and things I'm reading so I never get stuck in just my perspective.
 – Katylin

I have a plaque on my desk with Colossians 3:23-24 written on it. Some days I have to remind myself I work for God not man—WHATEVER I do—this includes serving or leading in areas I don't normally work (it is hard). I also have a group for accountability.
 – Susan

I remind myself who I am beyond my title regularly. When you imagine yourself without your title it reminds you that you aren't your title. I ask God at least yearly if this is where He wants me and then listen. Remember, your family only knows you as you, so be the person you want to be around them. Your kids don't care about your title, but they do care how you treat people. – Dianne

I remind myself often about who called me and empowers me. – Natalie

I remember that my role on staff is an expression of my calling but that my calling will go with me wherever I am placed. I guess for me it's knowing what I am called to and knowing that calling has the highest priority and lives itself out no matter where I work. – Heather

Know how to rest well and define what sabbath could look like in your context so you are less likely to develop a Messiah complex. – Evi

QUICK *Tips*

Here are some practical tips to help you avoid being defined by the title you have in the ministry:

✓ Determine your core values.

✓ Spend some time in prayer and seek God's response to who you are.

✓ Ask a few friends to pray with you as you seek to see yourself as God sees you.

✓ If you are struggling with this whole idea, then consider talking to a trusted friend or even a licensed Christian Counselor.

  ✓ This has been a huge part of my health and healing over the years in ministry and I highly suggest having a counselor you can trust to help you work through some of the topics we will be addressing in the book.

✓ Consider investing in a Christian Life Coach, specifically someone with ministry experience, who can help guide you as you move forward.

  ✓ A counselor will help you work on the stuff from your past that might be holding you back while a life coach will help you strategically move forward.

Chapter 2

YOU ARE MORE THAN JUST: THE SKILLS YOU BRING TO THE MINISTRY

You Gotta Know Yourself

We've already talked about the fact that you are more than just the title you have in ministry so now let's talk about the skills you bring to the ministry. You are more than just the things you are good at. If you are a communicator, you are more than just the things you communicate. If you are an administrative person, you are more than just the administrative stuff you do.

This is why it is really important to know who you are. It is far too easy to be swayed, morphed, or manipulated (not necessarily on purpose, but simply because of the culture of your organization) to be the one thing you are really good at doing. Let's take for instance the fact that I am a really good note taker. This is because like Dory in *Finding Nemo*, I tend to get very distracted—especially in long meetings. I take voracious notes throughout meetings to keep myself engaged, and as a side benefit in my more "seasoned" years, it helps to remember specific details that I might accidentally forget.

Knowing that about myself allows me the opportunity to know where my strengths and my weaknesses are as a person and as a leader. I am a big believer in personality tests like Meyers-Briggs, StrengthsFinder, DISC, etc. They can be extremely useful and beneficial to you in fully understanding your leadership style, yourself as a person, and can help you as you learn to develop your spiritual gifts from the Lord.

Here's my one caveat to these tests—please don't use them as a crutch. Don't say, "Well, . . . I'm this so that means this, or I will never be this because I'm that." The results of personality tests are not meant to be an inhibition or an excuse, but rather, a magnifying glass that you can use to really dig in and know the skills you bring to the table. The most important person, and maybe the hardest person, you will ever lead is yourself, so make sure you get a good and clear picture of who you are and your gifts.

> "If your actions create a legacy that inspires others to dream more, learn more, do more and become more, then, you are an excellent leader." -Dolly Parton[2]

Take the Time to Know Your Spiritual Gifts and Natural Gifts

Back in the seventies and eighties, school was all about working to better the classes and grades in which you struggled the most. It always felt to me like there was some unwritten goal that we were to be the best at everything. This resulted in spending an inordinate amount of time working to raise the grades of the subjects we simply were not good at while doing the minimum on the things that came easier to us.

Over time and after years of trying hard, I've come to find out that we are not wired to be the best at everything.[3] There's a great quote by Simon Sinek that says, "We can't be good at everything. If we were, there would be no need for teams."[4] We can be good at many things but being the best at everything really just makes us the best at nothing. You know the old saying, "jack of all trades, master of none." That's a great way to look at this idea of trying to be the best at everything. So, if we don't have to be great at everything, how do we get it all done?

We bring people around us to fill in the gaps of our leadership gifts and skills. Here's a good example: I am a vision and idea person, but the details can sometimes get lost on me, so I make sure to have people on my team that are detailed. That way when I have some great big pie in the sky idea, they can help me see that to make that happen it's going to take x, y, and z. If I hadn't had the input of someone detail-oriented, I may have only thought of a, b, and c before moving on without even realizing there was an x, y, and z to be done. Everyone's gifts work together to get things done.

I know that as a female leader in the ministry you already have some idea about how the body of Christ works, but I would be remiss if we didn't just take a few minutes to walk through this together. I love that the Bible digs into this so beautifully, basically saying that no one gift is more important than any other and that we need all the gifts to work together to make a whole.

There are two places in the Bible I'd love for us to read through to get a better understanding. The first passage is in Romans 12:3-8 (ESV) where it says,

> For by the grace given to me I say to everyone among you not to think of himself more highly than he ought to think, but to think with sober judgment, each according to the measure of faith that God has assigned. For as in one body we have many members, and the members do not all have the same function, so we, though many, are one body in Christ, and individually members one of another. Having gifts that differ according to the grace given to us, let us use them: if prophecy, in proportion to our faith; if service, in our serving; the one who teaches, in his teaching; the one who exhorts, in his exhortation; the one who contributes, in generosity; the one who leads, with zeal; the one who does acts of mercy, with cheerfulness.

The second passage is 1 Corinthians 12:4-7 (ESV) where it says,

> Now there are varieties of gifts, but the same Spirit; and there are varieties of service, but the same Lord; and there are varieties of activities, but it is the same God who empowers them all in everyone. To each is given the manifestation of the Spirit for the common good.

When you take the time to read through Scripture and let it truly sink into your heart it really is an incredible gift along with the specific gift(s) God has given you. So how do you know what gift(s) you have been given to offer in service?

This is where it's important to take some time to ask God to show you. Then you can go right to Scripture and find out what gifts are listed. Next, you can find a spiritual gifts test online. Most of them are free and they can help you zero in on what God has given you. It usually doesn't take long to take these tests, and they are a good place to start.

It's also helpful to note that every believer is given at least one gift. You can have more gifts and your gifts might grow or even change as you mature. In looking back at the first spiritual gifts test I took years ago compared to the one that I took recently as a more seasoned believer, I can see some similarities, but I can also see that some new gifts have been developed over the years.

It would also be great to talk to a trusted pastor, leader, or friend who knows you and ask them what they see in you. Sometimes it's hard to discern what we are naturally good at and what God has supernaturally given us as a spiritual gift, so be patient with the process. It'll be worth the wait to get a clear picture of your gift(s). It's helpful for you to know the difference between your natural talent, which are things we are good at on our own and can be successful with in our own strength, and spiritual gifts, which are for the benefit of God's Kingdom, are gifted to us by His Holy Spirit, and only useful through His strength.

Once you've started to uncover your gift(s), it's time to get out there and use them. God created you and there is no one like you. In His divine design of you, He created you to meet a specific need and purpose in the world and in the body of Christ (generally seen as the local church).

If your gift is service, then look for ways to serve behind the scenes. If your gift teaching or leadership and you are hiding behind some other gift (like service), then it's time to get on that stage (so to speak) and stop shrinking back.

When you step up and use your gifts you are doing exactly what He created you to do. For me, being seen as a "bossy" little girl in 4th grade was the first hint of the leadership gifts He has given me. It's now up to me to use that gift in stewardship for the Kingdom.

My gifts are what make *me* unique.

Your gifts are what make *you* unique.

It's Time to Invest in Your Leadership

Once you have taken the time to dig in and find out what your spiritual gifts are, then do an inventory of your leadership by taking one of the leadership and personality quizzes. Ministry—in any capacity or given any gift or role—is leadership. The next step for you to take is to invest in your leadership. Later in the book we are going to spend a lot more time specifically talking about owning your leadership and gifts, but here we're going to talk specifically about doing what it takes to develop and grow the gifts and abilities that you've been given.

Here's some inside information: you must be intentional with how you are going to invest in yourself. On top of that, developing as a leader needs to be a priority. No one is going to advocate for you as much as you will (Okay, so maybe your spouse, best friend, or parents will care too, but you know what I mean). If I, as a leader, don't pursue the growth opportunities around me then I am essentially choosing to stay stagnant. Ouch. Neither I, nor anyone reading this book, wants to stay stagnant in their growth.

I get it, though. Depending on where you are in the org chart or in your leadership career that can sound like it is easier said than done but think about it honestly for a minute. If you want to grow and develop, your first step might just be standing up and making the ask with your supervisor or ministry leader. It might feel scary to advocate for yourself, but it doesn't have to be when you are truly seeking to grow.

In the early years it was harder to advocate for myself and make the ask. But I would pick out one big conference a year that I really thought would benefit my development as well as the organization I was working with at the time. I wanted it to be a win-win—for me and for them.

As I became a little more seasoned in my life and experience it was a lot easier for me to 1) advocate for myself, 2) find a win-win for the organization, and 3) make a big ask, plus some. This wasn't so because I am greedy, but simply because I am a big believer in you don't have if you don't ask. I am generally going to ask for a little bit more than I really want, you know . . . swing for the fences, but also give plenty of room for negotiation. Again, it needs to be a win-win for both parties for it to make sense, but I've learned that it's rare to encounter a leadership team that simply did not want to invest in their leaders. They might respond that it's not the right time, financially feasible, or there may be an event, conference, or training they would prefer I go to instead, but they've never said no because they don't want to develop me.

And historically, there were four specific areas of focus that have been pivotal to my leadership development. The first is attending conferences and training events. There are so many wonderful, amazing, and incredible events out there right now that it would be impossible to list them all. In each stage of my leadership, and in every role along the way, there were specific and targeted training opportunities (whether it was in Kids' Ministry, Women's Ministry, Church Communications, Speaking,

Church Administration or otherwise). I would highly recommend digging into some training specific for your role that will help take you to the next level of your leadership development.

The second thing is coaching. I have been in group coaching as well as individual executive coaching with some of the best and brightest leaders in ministry. Find a coach that you admire, respect, look up to, and can learn from. Remember, though, you are not trying to be their friend. Of course, this doesn't mean they won't become your friend. You just want to make sure you select someone who will help you learn and grow along the way. Each of the three women who have coached me over the years have become dear friends and trusted mentors . . . so it can happen that you get amazing coaching and a new friend at the same time. After many years of coaching women in the ministry I have been blessed to be able to call many of them dear friends of mine as well as clients.

The third thing is Christian counseling. This is one that really isn't talked about enough in the ministry and yet it has been vital for my growth, development, and health as a church leader for more than twenty years. I tell women in ministry all the time that my counselors have been one of the best investments that I've made in my personal and professional life. I go every month, no matter what. Life is hard enough and then you add in the demands and pressure of ministry, and it helps to have a trusted professional that can help me process and move through tough seasons. Let's face it, ministry thrusts us into people's highest moments (celebrations, weddings, and birthdays) as well as their lowest moments (divorce, death, and addiction). My counselor has helped me to remain healthy so that I can continue to serve out of the overflow instead of being buried under the heaviness of what I do.

The fourth thing that is pivotal to my leadership development was getting a two-day life plan done. Investing in a life plan was a major turning point for me in my ministry. After years of doing "all the things" because I could do them, it gave me the focus and intentionality to really narrow it all down and concentrate on the zone of what I could uniquely do (my why). Over the course of the two days, I found my why, my personal core values, and a very clear framework to filter through all my career and life decisions that kept coming into my life. It was like a Nehemiah 6:3 (ESV) moment, "I am doing a great work and I cannot come down" to all the distractions that were keeping me from doing the thing God created me to do.

I know it can seem like a hefty investment to do a two-day life plan, but if I could encourage you in this it would be that it is 100% worth it. I did my life plan with Kadi Cole, Founder & Lead Consultant at Kadi Cole & Company (I would highly recommend her) and she helped dig out of me the things that I didn't even realize were uniquely me. And when I finally stopped to see it all out in the open, it radically transformed the trajectory of my ministry in the best possible way.

Here are some practical solutions for and knowing yourself and developing the gifts you bring to the table:

Know yourself:

» What are your strengths? If you've taken a personality test, what did it say? What did you agree with and what stood out to you the most?

  » These tests can be a magnifying glass that you can use to really dig in deeply to understanding and implementing your gifts.

» Work within your giftedness and bring on other team members or volunteers to help fill in on your weaknesses. You cannot and should not try to do it all and be it all to everyone.

Know your gifts:

» If you have taken a spiritual gifts inventory test, what is your top gift(s)?

  » https://spiritualgiftstest.com

  » https://gifts.churchgrowth.org/spiritual-gifts-survey

» If it was taken years ago, consider taking one now to see if your gift(s) have changed.

» Using your gift(s) to maximize your impact in your organization doesn't just happen by accident, make sure you are intentionally looking for opportunities to utilize your gifts in a way that supports your organization.

Invest in your leadership:

» Advocate for yourself and your leadership development to make sure it is a win-win for the organization.

» Coaching is a great next step to your leadership development. Getting a chance to learn and grow from a more seasoned ministry leader will not only help you, but it will also benefit your organization as well.

» Consider adding a "book" line to your ministry budget. This will allow you the flexibility to continually learn and grow as you lead.

Real Ministry Chick Experience
from Cathie Ostapchuk

If you are anything like me, chances are you have spent a third, half, or even more of your life trying to please people. In my work as a leadership catalyst, I have met very few female leaders who have, more often than not, looked at their sphere of influence and set about making sure they could meet everyone's perceived needs before they did the work of exploring what they could uniquely bring into those environments.

Often I, and maybe you, have asked, "What do you need from me?" rather than declaring confidently, "This is what you can expect from me." We rarely have enough confidence in our strengths and unique gifting that our yes's are given away with little thought. The ways of showing up that are unique to our one and only selves rarely have a chance to shine in the limelight since we have kept them hidden while being at the beck and call of other people's personal and ministry expectations.

Girls, I am this woman. Right out of the gate from Bible college and two degrees and seminary later into a ministry environment, I learned how to take the easy road to likeability by saying yes. I threw out a frequent yes to pastors, peers, congregations, and friends because I thought that in ministry this was the baseline expectation and people liked me more. Isn't that what every female leader wants?

My yes to others created havoc within my soul as time and time again, I denied my own desires to serve in the ways that I was passionate about in order to please others.

Very often as women leaders, when we are wrestling with wanting to do the right thing and at the same time listening to the whispers of God in our heart, stress and anxiety result. We somehow know we are failing to be true to our very souls and defaulting on ourselves. This can result in defining moments—either of plateauing, burning out, or falling off the leadership journey entirely.

I found myself trapped in an elevator one day. Running in to the elevator with several yes jobs to fulfill,

I found myself pressing the button hard and fast to parking level so I could get in my car and keep running to do all the things people were expecting of me. This crazy pace of running became my life and was on repeat 7 days a week, month after month, year after year.

The elevator door did not open when I got to parking level. I kept hitting the open button with more and more force, until I heard a whisper in my soul, "Cathie, that's not your door." I turned around and realized it was a double-sided elevator and the door was open behind me.

I realized in that moment I needed to be a different girl leaving the elevator than the people-pleasing, frantic one that entered it. It took me a few years of exploring how God had gifted me uniquely and to learn to say a healthy yes and a confident no to the expectations of those around me. I learned to save 60% of my yes responses for those things that were in the area of my unique ability and called on my God-given birthright strengths. And I learned to slow down and serve in my own healthy cadence in ministry.

We are to pay close attention to how God has gifted us for ministry. Jesus Christ has wired each of us to function in the world for His glory. Jesus, by whom and for whom we were made, and by whom and for whom we are being redeemed, has uniquely wired each of us to live and serve in unique ways.

It is the gospel part of our personhood. I call this area of unique wiring and service, the 'grace zone'.

Darrell Johnson, in *The Glory of Preaching*, says it like this:

> Gifted is the more usual term. Charismatized is the more literal biblical term; charismatized, from charisma, meaning 'gift of grace.' Every member of the body of Christ in the world has been charismatized, graciously endowed by the Holy Spirit to perform a unique function in the church and in the world. That gifting goes so deep within us that it contributes to our identity—and constitutive of our being. It is not so much that we have a gift; rather it is that we are a gift.[5]

For the female leader, this is a harder concept not only to grasp but to act on. It means being willing to show up strong, having done the work of unpacking your birthright gifts, and boldly offering them to your ministry environment. It means shaping your environment to make room for what only you can bring and influencing others to do the same. Again, it is knowing the sound of your healthy yes and confident no. It doesn't mean there won't be times when all team members need to pitch in and pull together—but most of the time it means all of you bringing what only you can bring. Men do this more naturally and they don't diminish their strengths. Women more naturally believe we must work on our weaknesses.

Resist the urge. Learn the wonder of what God has fashioned in you. The work of offering your graced self, humbly and confidently, is your work and your greatest gift to the world.

Reflect on these stunning words from Stephen Covey as you begin to understand how fearfully and wonderfully you have been created. Steward those gifts to serve the world God has positioned you in for such a time as now.

> The power to discover your voice lies in the potential that was bequeathed you at birth. Latent and undeveloped, the seeds of greatness were planted. You were given magnificent birth-gifts—talents, capacities, privileges, intelligences, opportunities—that would remain largely unopened except through your own decision and effort. Open these gifts. Learn what taps your talents and fuels your passion—that rises out of a great need in the world that you feel drawn by conscience to meet—therein lies your voice, your calling, your soul's code.[6]

I believe in you.

Chick CHAT

Real, practical advice on being a female leader in the ministry to make sure that you don't shrink back or hide your gifts and skills.

You need accountability partners to hold you accountable. – Roslyn

Live for the applause of the One with "nailed scarred hands" rather than the applause of man. – Lori

I remind women that when we don't open and use our gifts it's like a slap in the face to our gift-giver. Our gifts showcase His glory not ours so don't be afraid to use them! – Kelly

I invite others to come sit at the table of leadership with me. And I remind myself that every time I walk fully in my gifts and skills, I am encouraging another woman to do the same, especially younger women.
– Angela

Always keep learning and exploring new opportunities to understand how your gifts fit into God's purpose for how He has uniquely designed you! Don't box yourself in - be ready to serve where He leads. – Shari

Say "YES!" to Jesus every morning all over again so that I'm empowered afresh to use the gifts and skills HE gave me to help others and, ultimately glorify Him.

The more present I am with Him, the more He guides me and shows me ways every day on how and where to share my gifts. – Kristen

Keep remembering the moment, place, and space you knew that the Lord was calling you into ministry. Because the call of Christ is what will encourage, strengthen, and sustain you in the tough times and what will keep you humble and focused when pride threatens to take credit in your ministries. – Rehana

Never apologize for having a different idea or suggestion. – Carol

Know and understand that your gifts were not given for you. Your gifts are meant to be shared! God blesses us to bless the nations as He did with Abraham in Gen 12. Be bold and courageous with your gifts and steward them well for a higher kingdom purpose! – Tiffany

A friend shared this with me at a key time and it is on my computer desktop as a "stickie" constant reminder: "Rest in your God-breathed worth. Stop holding your breath, hiding your gifts, ducking your head, dulling your roar, distracting your soul, stilling your hands, quieting your voice, and satiating your hunger . . . Stop waiting for someone else to say that you count, that you matter, that you have worth, that you have a voice, a place, that you are called. Don't you know, darling? The One who knit you together in your mother's womb is the one singing these words over you? You are chosen!" (Author unknown) – Julie

I've had to learn how to discover when fear is holding me back. The way I see fear most often expressed in my life is I'm the one trying to control the outcome of a situation. When I am in control of everything, I am limited in how far I can go. I have to surrender the outcome to God in order to have "Nothing is impossible with God" kind of results. – Stephanie

Chapter 3

YOU ARE MORE THAN JUST: THE ONLY FEMALE AT THE TABLE—BEING THE TOKEN FEMALE

What happens when you are the only woman at "the table"?

What does "at the table" even mean?

Honestly, why are people always talking about "the table" anyway?

For a quick and simple description of "the table" we'll keep it basic. The table is the place in your organization where all the big decisions are made. Whoever sits at the table is part of the decision-making team of your organization, and if you are the highest-ranking female leader on staff, you might be the only woman that sits at the table. And you may be invited to sit at the table because, chances are, you are one of few women being represented, which means you are the voice for yourself and any other women in your organization.

First of all, let me say this, I get it. I have been the only woman at the table in several ministries over the years and it is both humbling, exciting, terrifying, and many other emotions at the same time. There is a lot of pressure at the table and I'm sure, like me, you wish there were other women joining you.

There is a delicate balance to your position as the only woman at the decision-making table and yes, you might want to tread lightly until you get the lay of the land. Your first time in those meetings might be a time of observation to learn the dynamics of those meetings, but do not shrink back and hide. Don't let yourself be the one who sets up the coffee, brings the snacks, or even takes the notes. That is not why you are there (unless, of course, that is why you are there, but you know what I mean).

If you have been invited to be at the table, you are there on your own leadership abilities and your role within the organization. At that table you are the expert in whatever team you lead or work on, so it is up to you to advocate for your team and to speak clearly about the situation being discussed. You are not doing anyone any favors if you sit at the table and never speak up. If you do that then chances are they will stop inviting you to those meetings. Your voice needs to be heard.

If you want to think about it from a 30,000-foot view, your voice, as a woman, represents roughly about 60% of your church, ministry, or organization. This means it is imperative that you use your voice to represent your team, experiences, and thoughts. Women see, feel, and sense things a little differently than men, so we should not ignore them simply because we don't want to rock the boat.

Being on a team where everyone leads within their giftedness and uses their voice to be an advocate for those they are called to lead is good, healthy, and extremely important. There have been times when I would see something in a meeting that every one of us was looking at and saw in a different light and brought it up only to have a giant "aha!" moment happen within the group. In fact, had I not shared it, the issue probably would have been completely overlooked and problems would have grown over time. The table cannot—and should not—be stocked with all the same demographics because this means that we will miss out on the voices of all the people represented within our organization.

It is not likely you will be responsible for deciding who gets invited to the table. But because you have been invited, you need to leverage the uniqueness of your femininity while making sure you are leading well from your seat. There are some helpful ways to make sure that you are leading well while you are the only woman at the table. You are a woman. That is 100% fact, so you do not have to try to be more like the guys to fit in at that meeting. But it's fair to acknowledge that women, by nature, tend to be more emotional than men, so you also don't want to be an emotional mess in that meeting either. Yes, we are women, we have emotions, and we can sometimes feel so deeply and passionately that we might cry or even raise our voices in a meeting (I'm speaking for a friend, of course).

In the right place, time, and context, emotions are a very natural response to what's going on in and around you. You express yourself through your emotions. Don't let anyone tell you otherwise. It's only an issue or a concern if you get in a situation where your emotions get the better of you and cause undue stress or anxiety, either within yourself or those around you while it is happening.

The truth of the matter is, though, that having a moment of an unmanaged emotion is going to happen. How you handle it really sets the tone and helps you to recover from it as well as allows everyone in the room to know that this is a rare occurrence and that you are a professional and can pull it back together.

Emotions are not bad. After all, God gave us emotions. Jesus was emotional as well:

» He wept (John 11:35).

» He got angry (Mark 10:14).

» He turned over tables (John 2:15).

» He had compassion (Mark 1:41).

» He was filled with joy (Luke 10:21).

If you are in a meeting and your emotions start to get out of control, especially for the situation, then the best thing you can do is excuse yourself so that you can go and collect yourself. Take a moment to pray. Give it to God and ask Him for His peace or direction as you prepare to go back to the meeting. Rinse your face and put yourself back together. Finally, walk back in the room and apologize if you were out of line or overly emotional. You don't have to go into full detail as to why you responded as you did, and you don't need to dwell on it either. The best thing you can do at that moment is to pull yourself back together as a professional and then get back to work. This is especially necessary as a female leader that works in a predominantly male-dominated environment because we are needed, our voice is important, and the ministry is better when we work together.

It's important to check your emotions and make sure they are in sync with what is really going on in the meeting or on the topic. There are times (we know this) that our emotions can be a little out of whack, whether it is a physical or hormonal issue, personal matters at home, or even an earlier exchange with a colleague that didn't go as planned and you simply have not had enough time to process. It happens! Goodness knows that I have experienced this more than a few times but remember the bigger issues at hand. As one of the only female leaders, it's vital for your voice to be heard effectively and without distraction.

This is not the time for the matter to be taken personally (even though it can be at times); it's the time to be the professional leader that God created and equipped you to be. There's no room for the silent treatment, a scowl on your face or any other non-verbal cue communicating you are not happy. You can be unhappy about something and still be a professional. I would never suggest you need to hide your emotions, but I will say that we have a responsibility to get past our own personal stuff to get to the bigger issues at hand. While our emotions are not bad, they just may need to be processed later in private with a trusted colleague, friend, or your family. You want to be able to keep doing the work that you are called to do in that room with that team.

You can be a strong female leader, have emotions, make mistakes, and still lead confidently. As a matter of fact, we need to see more female leaders being a good strong influence. This doesn't mean you are expected to be perfect because no one is righteous, not even one (Romans 3:10) but it does mean you are willing to be real and authentic while making the effort to keep trying to do better.

It's also extremely important for you as a female leader to maximize the things that you know or are aware of as a woman. This can include something as simple as having access to the school calendar and thinking through no school days, holidays, spring break, and teacher workdays when planning the ministry calendar. You would be surprised at just how tightly leadership works to make sure the ministry calendar coincides with the school year calendar. You know why? That's when people get in or back into a rhythm and routine and when they are creating those rhythms for their families for school they can and often do the same when it comes to church.

For example, as a woman you might notice that there is spring break at the same time the team wants to do a great big all church event that week. Chances are that a good portion of your congregation might be traveling that week so it wouldn't be a good time to plan an event of that size. Sounds simple enough, but in every church leadership team I have been a part of, I am almost always the one that points out these kinds of school calendar conflicts. I don't even have school-aged kids any more, but I know that today's family runs off the school calendar, so I make sure to get one every year so that I can make sure we are planning in congruence with the school year instead of against it.

What happens though, when you are the only female leader and most of your meetings are with men? How do you still be uniquely you, but also speak in a way that is direct? This is not the time to beat around the bush or give long drawn-out explanations or stories. I know, I love a good story too, but there is work to be done here, so let's stick to the highlights.

I was at a conference decades ago and one of the speakers talked about this specific topic of leading as a woman in a staff full of men. I will never forget one of the things that was mentioned. She said, when communicating with men: stick to the bullet points in your emails, meetings, notes, etc. You can always give all the other data and info if it is requested, but most of the time stick to the facts.

This interested me so much I remember having a conversation with my husband about it. He's a data, facts, systems type of guy and when I told him what was said he immediately said an enthusiastic "YES!" His next response surprised me and helped me understand something I had been struggling with and didn't even realize it. I always sent over a ton of facts and data to back up whatever email or info I was sending to my senior leaders. He said, "I trust you (or whomever sent the email with the information). I hired you to do that job, so if, in your professional opinion you said to do this or that, then that is all I need to know."

His statement shook me. In my inexperience of being the only woman at the table I had subconsciously decided that I needed to "prove" to the others that I belonged there, so I spent extra time trying to justify and verify the information I was sharing with them. I realized now, though, all they really needed and wanted was the bullet points.

This realization totally revolutionized my communication. The leadership knew I did my due diligence, but they didn't necessarily need to see all of it to verify it themselves. It was my recommendation (unless more information was requested) that they desired. The extra data just crowds out the main point of your communication which could potentially keep them from reading it.

Simply put, with the speed at which we all move and the amount of responsibility we all carry, most people (especially men) skim to determine the bottom line, so when there is a long report or email there is a higher likelihood that 1) they will not completely read it or 2) they will put it off longer to respond until there is more time to read it fully. Either way, communication starts to break down. Make this a win-win for everyone. Stick to the facts and save the stories for later.

Also, before I forget, there are things you will need to think about as a female leader at the table and one of those things is how you will dress, accessorize, and everything in between. I am by no means advocating for stodgy, uncomfortable, or dressing like one of the guys. I think it is a beautiful gift to be a woman and I love the complexity and freedom there is to find our own style and shine as God created you to shine.

Specifically, if you are going to be "on stage" at any time or with a microphone our outfits and accessories can be distracting at times—not because of what we wear, but simply because they can keep people from hearing what we say. For example, I love pretty, dangly earrings, but if I have a lav microphone (that goes from behind my ear to my cheek) then chances are my earrings are going to rub on the mic and cause undue distraction and background noise.

Also, if you wear a white shirt on stage you can be pretty sure that it will end up being see through. This is not a great idea if you are trying to get people to take you seriously as a leader. Whether you wear skirts, dresses, jeans, or shirts, all of it can be carefully thought through and planned out from your vantage point on the stage. I know it's weird and uncomfortable to even "go there" in this conversation, but as a female leader in the Church, you are going to want to be ahead of this instead of learning it the hard way.

As if having to think through what you are wearing while on stage isn't enough, there is another unique challenge for female leaders, and that is establishing boundaries with the opposite sex, both those you work with on staff and those you might lead. The fact of the matter is that we really do need both men and women leading within their giftedness. We are one body working together for the good of our organization and as believers we are one body working together for the good of God our Father and His will for us here on earth. There is no greater feeling than when we are all working within our giftedness, encouraging each other along the journey and working to serve our community. This is why boundaries are good for you and good for the rest of the team. Don't put yourself in a situation where there could be speculation about your behavior with a man on your team. Unfortunately, in today's world, speculation can be traded for truth even when it's not. Take time to consider what safety steps you need to take to keep things professional and take precaution. I hate to even say it because women and men should be able to lead together without there being any weirdness, but in the world we live in currently, this isn't always the case.

Real Ministry Chick Experience

from Kristin Fry

Having a seat of influence at the boys' table.

I'd never given much thought to leading in a room full of men . . . until I found myself leading only men.

But let me back up.

I was born and raised in California. I bring that up because I often wonder if because of the early rise in female leadership in notable companies, including large Christian organizations, on the West Coast, I almost never faced discrimination in the workplace based on my gender. Gender was not a topic of conversation in the early years of my career. I grew up with two working parents, as did all of my friends. As far as I was concerned, there were no glass ceilings for me.

As an intern in my early twenties, I had both men and women in positions of authority invest in me and I was given every opportunity that the men were given. I had a speaking career that was birthed in my mid-twenties. An older man sitting in the audience during one of my gigs approached me after the fact, gave me a genuine compliment followed up by, "But I'm not sure how I feel about women preaching." To be honest, I assumed in part that he was joking because I didn't realize there were people who actually still believed that women shouldn't preach. I shrugged it off and went on with my life. Because of my larger context, comments like these left me relatively unfazed.

My career took twists and turns over the years and eventually led me to the South. It was in the South where I learned that people play by different rules in the workplace. Gender started to matter in certain situations, and what seemed so clear to me regarding my leadership—seemed to be not as clear to other people. It was all very fascinating to me.

But what was even more fascinating to me was that I made the decision to own who I was, to not shy away from my skill set and wiring because I am a female, and to keep moving forward. Even when my gender was called into question. I let it roll off my back like water over a duck's feathers. This was different from other women who grew up in the South. And I think that saved me. That mindset was, and still is, the biggest piece of leadership advice I have to offer to young women stepping into a man's world.

Leadership is mental.

It was in my late thirties when I found myself leading a team of all men. All married men, at that. Mind you, I was the only single person in the room, so being single and female was potentially a recipe for disaster in the South. Before my first day,

I found myself questioning everything. I wasn't in California anymore. This was the South—the South where these things mattered.

But on that first day, I gave myself a pep talk. I reminded myself that the context didn't matter. My skill set, experience, and wiring weren't going to change because I was in a different geographical location. I was capable and had every reason to be confident. I walked into my first meeting committed to being kind but clear, to ask good questions, listen well, and lead. And that's exactly what I did.

For the duration of my time with that team, our dynamics and relationships were top-notch. And on my last day with them, I asked them about those dynamics. We had open and honest communication and I was curious what they thought, if anything, of being led by a woman. I told them that I had never experienced anything but respect from Day 1 from each of them and wanted to know why that was. One by one, the men told me some version of, "Good leadership is good leadership. You can either lead or you can't and that has nothing to do with gender. If you had walked in here hesitant or questioning yourself, we would have as well. But you didn't. Besides, you had a reputation that precedes you, so we already had an idea of your track record."

And there it was. The most valuable piece of feedback I've ever received. **Good leadership is**

good leadership. And I held the power to hijack my own career by telling a story in my own head that I should be doubted exclusively for being a woman. But I didn't do that. After all, men don't walk into a room and wonder what everyone thinks of their gender, so why should I?

Whether male or female, you have a responsibility to study, learn, and practice all the things that make up a good leader. And then do it. If the calling on your life is to lead, then don't let the exterior context thwart that. So much of leadership is mental gymnastics and the stories we tell ourselves about what people may or may not be thinking. And if we allow those stories to dominate our decisions about leadership, we'll take ourselves out of the game before we even get started.

You have every right to a position of authority just like anyone else. Don't let the mental game beat you. Step into that room with confidence and just lead.

Chick CHAT

Real, practical advice on being a female leader in the ministry to communicate and lead well when you're the only woman in the room.

Avoid saying, "I feel . . ." Instead say, "I believe . . ." or "I think . . ." – Penny

Don't frequently wait until after most others have voiced their opinion before voicing your own. – Marlena

Cultivate a good sense of humor. Listen well and take initiative in contributing. Ask the Lord to help you to be both strong and vulnerable. Seek to grow in self-awareness so that you carry that awareness into the room with you. For me, it works to be gracious and also very honest and direct about my boundaries and what I can and cannot do (clarity). When addressing things that put the ego of another on the line, frame it as optimistically as possible. In other words, speak the truth, but convey hope and a doable path forward. Under promise, over deliver. – Heather

Avoid apologizing or offering justification such as "it's not perfect" before giving a presentation. Men tend to laugh off or at least hear out half-baked ideas from other men. However, it gives a great excuse to not take you seriously as a woman. – Marlena

Believe the best of those sitting around you. Even if you perceive the space you've been given as an afterthought or a small step in inclusivity, trust that God has placed you there for a reason. You have something valuable to bring to the table and it's important not to allow insecurity to silence your opportunity. (Ahem . . . preaching to myself . . .)

– Crystal

1. Your voice matters. Don't let someone make you think otherwise. You are at the table on purpose, so don't let intimidation into your heart, mind, or soul or even in the room. 2. In response to ideas, consider asking the question, "How would a new mom or elderly person or single person or fill in the blank person experience our event, service, _____?"
It helps get everyone in the room to put themselves in someone else's shoes which is taught and intentional, it is not caught. Likely you will add or subtract something from the plan, so people experience and feel what you hope for them to experience and feel. – Dianne

Let go of the weight of feeling like you have to represent "all women." When someone asks you "What do women think?" Lightly respond with "I have no idea! But I can tell you what I think." Also, laugh and let other people know it's okay to laugh. One time I was in a prayer meeting when someone prayed that we'd all be made "mighty men of God."

Someone else prayed that I, in particular, would be a mighty man of God and then cracked up. We all did . . . it was good for us all. – Pam

Don't apologize for speaking. You are there because your voice is necessary. – Amanda

Talk in bullet points and use "organization" words instead of "family" words. Use these words when talking about leadership: org chart, job description, role, leadership development, projects, opportunity (instead of the word "problem"), progress, task, etc. Use language that doesn't attack their character/skill level. For example: "Can we get clarity?" instead of "You aren't making any sense." And stay out of the weeds because not every thought needs a story to explain its why. Charts and numbers that show results or comparisons are also a win! – Stephanie

I prep a handout of any additional information that they can read on their own outside of the meeting. This helps me feel like I gave all the pertinent information without needing to take the whole meeting to explain. Hit the highlights, answer questions. – Gena

*You don't have to impress anyone. You're at the table because God put you there. *Remember, because you are a woman specifically, you have a unique perspective to offer. – Tracy*

Be yourself. Be authentic. Don't be anyone other than who God made you to be. – Becky

Get to the point. Girl chat is all about the details . . . but in a leadership conversation, the moments count, so use them effectively. If you have a 60-minute meeting, don't take 12 minutes to explain your idea. – Meredith

1) It's hard to argue with excellent, professional work and preparation. Excellence lends credibility right off the bat. 2) My favorite Proverb is 25:15 (NIV), "A gentle tongue can break a bone." 3) Guys don't usually center their identity as a male in conversations (they don't have to) so don't feel the need to center your language around your femaleness. Work toward representation of women in your sphere as you want, but in decision-making spaces, speak as a leader first (who is also a woman); don't pigeonhole yourself as only relevant to what is considered female. I wasn't in a leadership role but did a lot of internal org advocacy as a women's empowerment specialist. Just a disclaimer. – Aria

1. Be biblically literate. Know the Word of God; act and advise accordingly in all matters; otherwise, you will undermine your calling and position.
2. You don't have to have the answer to every question that comes up in the meeting, but you should be the expert on your function. Demonstrate that you have a pulse on things and are on top of your plans. 3. Be a good team player. Be helpful to your other ministry colleagues. It builds good rapport. 4. Be the woman in the room. Your church staff

needs to hear a female perspective. 5. Be open to suggestions from your team. You don't have to ditch your plans, but you may want to modify some things based upon their feedback. No one is above having a blind spot. 6. Be on time. Be pleasant. Be engaged. And have a can-do spirit. Have fun. 7. Employ the fruit of the Spirit and showcase your high emotional intelligence quotient. You will have plenty of opportunities to do this as you know. 8. Love out loud. In the end, our main goal is to love people to Jesus, and minister in His Name. – Gina

You are more than likely making history in your church. Rather than look for role models, become one. Leave a legacy of someone who defined her role and owned it with excellence and integrity. Make eye contact and be over-prepared and decisive. Lead with a team mentality because the ultimate goal is the win for the whole. Make room at the table for other women. If you're doing your job well, the doors will open. – Susan

Speak up, don't shrink back. – Natalie

Earn your spot, but then own it. – Kathy

Don't change or adjust who you are in order to be accepted at the table. If this is necessary, you're at the wrong table. Go in with clear, concise ideas. Make room for other women at the table. – Bekah

Know your context. Use your understanding to frame communication with clarity and excellence. – Sara

Trust that God has called you and your calling is biblical. Walk in humility and courage. God will walk beside you each step of the way. – Debbie

I always loved being the only woman at the table. I don't know why. I was just always that girl growing up that loved hanging out with the guys. My advice would be when another woman FINALLY joins the table with you, don't be jealous. It's hard not to be jealous of other women because you do feel like there are so many spots open at the table. But remember that God's table is not limited. It's always growing. He has plenty of work for all women and there is no need to be jealous of someone else. You're unique and so is she. Both of you will be needed. – Rachael

Ask yourself, "How do I want to show up in this meeting?" and "How do I need to show up in this meeting?" Speak with courage and confidence. I frequently ask questions in order to get my point across. Also, use "I wonder" when challenging ideas: "I wonder if we are ignoring another perspective?" Or "I wonder if we have other options." – Michelle

Arrive early enough that you can pick your seat at the table. I try to be within 3 seats of the person who leads the meeting. Too often (especially if it's a big meeting) you can find yourself in no man's land of seats. If you are there to just listen, that's fine. But if you are there for input, you need to be close enough to be seen and heard. There is probably something in the subconscious too about how seriously a person's input is taken based on their proximity to the meeting leader. – Gena

This is crucial! Sit in the spot for the role you want to serve in the meeting. It's scientific! https://www. scienceofpeople.com/seating-arrangement/ – Janie

Find an ally in the meetings who understands that too often your voice will not be heard (Or find a man will pick up your idea, use it as his own, and everyone will think he's brilliant. Happens way too often). Ask them to repeat what you say and credit you. – Pam

Come into the room boldly. Don't slink in. Smile big and greet at least one person by name. Get there a few minutes early. Take up space visually. Spread out a bit. Agree with people you agree with out loud not just in your head, so the people can see and hear that you are an ally. Know your stuff! I try to be twice as prepared for a meeting as the next person. – Rebekah

1) Take the word "just" out of your vocabulary . . . "I just want to add . . . " "I just believe that . . . " 2) Be selective with the pen (or keyboard or marker) . . . a) If someone is needed to take notes to document what is being discussed so follow up can happen, don't volunteer to do that right away. Wait until you have established yourself as a contributor as well as a notetaker. b) If someone is needed to write on a white board, that is often a great place to be. Having the pen (marker) gives you the chance to facilitate or co-facilitate by asking clarifying questions and getting consensus as you write things on the board. (Re: 2a . . . this is also tricky with playing host (getting snacks, water, coffee). I had a mentor who is a female attorney tell me that she loves to play that role. But she waited several years after she had established her role before, she took on being hostess, too. She loves to serve people but wanted to make sure other women knew she was doing it out of her desire to do so and not because a woman should do those tasks.) – Janie

Real Ministry Chick Experience

from Rev. Dr. Candace M. Lewis

Today, I am inspired as I reflect upon my almost twenty-years as a Black woman in church leadership. Being the first, the only, one of a few, and now a part of the many women in church leadership has been a journey.

I discerned a call to ministry in 1991 when I was only 23 years old. I graduated from college a year earlier and returned home to spend a year working and trying to figure out what to do with my life. As a young woman, I had to admit at that time, I had only seen very few women in church leadership. Some were evangelists, preachers, and teachers. I only knew one woman who was an appointed senior pastor of a local church, and her name was Rev. Geraldine. Rev. Geraldine was the pastor of the Mt. Pleasant United Methodist church in Gainesville, Florida. I attended her church while I was in college and she had a very powerful presence, speaking voice and preaching a hope-filled message weekly.

During my exploration year after college, I was intentional about reading Scripture and desired to grow in my faith. I would set aside Wednesdays as a day to fast lunch and instead would go to a park during my break to read, study, journal, and reflect. One random Wednesday, as I was in the park a person walked up to me and handed me a book and said, "The Holy Spirit nudged me to give this to you." The book was called *Run to the Battle*. God used that book to help me take a "next faithful step" in hearing and answering a call to full time ministry. I shared this idea that God was "calling me" with my local church Pastor, Rev. Brown. Rev. Brown listened, prayed, and suggested I attend an event. When I arrived at the event, I was nervous and wasn't sure why I was there. When they announced the focus of the meeting, the speaker said, "You're called by God, now what?" I sat in the back and cried the entire time.

Several other serendipitous invitations came which continued to reassure me I was being "called" to ministry and now I wanted to be prepared. At the time, I couldn't "google" seminaries and research with ease what my next steps would be, but I knew I wanted to be trained. I heard about Gammon Theological Seminary as a graduate theological school, applied, and was accepted. In fall 1992, I relocated to Atlanta, Georgia to begin seminary. I was 24 years old, heading to the big city coming from a small town in Florida. Living in Atlanta was a life-changing experience. Everything was big! Prior to my move, I had never heard of or seen a "mega" church. In the 90's, churches were starting to grow to mega in size and impact. I joined a mega church near the seminary called Central United Methodist Church. From 1993-1996, I served as the youth and college ministries pastor at Central connecting with over a thousand members between two worship experiences weekly. I also met amazing young adults while attending seminary who were also answering their call to ministry, and together we were trained and are still lifelong friends.

In 1996, upon graduating from seminary, I was appointed by the Bishop of the Florida Conference of the United Methodist Church to start a new church. I was also ordained and appointed that year as a full-time pastor. I had no idea what a church planter did, nor did I know how to start a church from scratch. I was the first Black woman the conference had ever appointed to start a new church and the conference hadn't started a new Black church in over twenty years. There were no coaches, bootcamps, or books I could read to receive perspective on this new appointment as a young, female, who was also a beautiful single woman in ministry. I was the first and needed to learn how to be a pioneer. I found comfort in Scripture, especially the book of Esther.

Being a young woman answering a call to full time ministry, I was often met with opposition that said, "women should keep silent" in the churches. This is only a man's job. I had learned in seminary that some interpretations of the biblical text could be taken out of context. That text wasn't meant to "silence" women for all times. I found reassurance reading Esther 4:14 (NIV), "For if you remain silent at this time, relief and deliverance will arise for the Jews from another place, but you and your father's house will perish. Yet who knows whether you have come to the kingdom for such a time as this?" I have always felt like I was "called to the kingdom for such a time as this." I've always known I was called to speak and not keep silent. I had to learn to be courageous and confident as I grow in competence.

As a new pioneer and first woman to plant or start a new church in our conference, I learned that I might be the first in my own context but probably not the first ever to hear and answer this call to ministry. That's when I learned to look outside of my denominational tribe for mentors and resource leaders.

While in Atlanta, I learned of the Rev. Dr. Cynthia Hale, who was the founding pastor of the Ray of Hope Church in Atlanta, Georgia. I sent her an email and told her how overwhelmed I felt receiving this new appointment and asked if I could visit. She responded to my email agreeing I could shadow her for a day at no charge. This experience was life giving and affirming in my early days of being the first female church planter. Always remember as the "first" in your context you might be able to connect with another "first" in a different context. Meeting and seeing Dr. Hale leading a growing, thriving church assured me I could do it as well. The Ray of Hope Church had over five hundred members at the time with hundreds of people in mission and ministry weekly. Dr. Hale also hosted a Women in Ministry Conference yearly which convened Black Women who were theologians, pastors, teachers, writers, business professionals, and professors all in one place and space. I attended her conference and always left inspired, equipped, and encouraged to live out my call another year.

In June 1997, we launched the New Life Community United Methodist Church. In that first year some amazing people joined our launch team and together we started a new church. I served in that appointment for twelve years and wow! That was an amazing season of life and ministry leadership. I grew immensely as a person and as a leader. Those twelve years enabled me to build a solid foundation as a pastor, preacher, teacher, leader, visionary, innovator, and entrepreneur who happens to be a woman. I knew I was called by God to lead and serve. Luke 6:44 (ESV) says, "For each tree is known by its own fruit." When I and others evaluated my years of service and ministry, it was fruitful. New Life was impacting our local community. We started a pre-school and after school program. We worshipped weekly and grew disciples who served in mission and ministry throughout our community. We experienced much success and learned from our many failures, yet together we were making disciples of Jesus Christ and would be a part of transforming this world.

Serving in that appointment for twelve years was amazing, yet also during that time I experienced health challenges, burnout, exhaustion, personal and professional loss, and grief. I learned the importance of clarity of calling and serving in the areas of your natural strength as a woman in church leadership. We need to be clear about our God-given gifts, talents, and strengths. Serving where you are gifted is energizing and life giving. Always adapting to the demands of the ministry context can lead to burnout and a loss of joy. With the help of a counselor and a coach, I learned that my calling was not only to my current ministry context. When I became open to other places God might be able to use me, my coach presented information about a new national ministry that was beginning in our denomination and encouraged me to apply for the position. I interviewed and was offered the position and moved to Nashville, Tennessee to begin my next season of life and ministry.

I started my new ministry appointment as a consultant, coach, and strategist in new church planting at Path1 in Nashville, Tennessee in 2009. In 2012, I applied and was promoted as the first woman and Black woman to serve as the executive director of the Path1 new church starts division at the General Board of Discipleship, a general agency of the United Methodist Church. This season enabled me to travel across every jurisdiction in our denomination resourcing the work of church planters. Imagine the joy I experienced daily being able to resource church planters and teams in ways I was not able to be resourced.

This season of my life was restorative and redemptive. 1 Peter 5:10 (ESV) says, "And after you have suffered for a little while, the God of all grace, who has called you to his eternal glory in Christ, will himself restore, support, strengthen, and establish you." God used this season to restore, support, strengthen, and most of all establish me as a woman called by God to lead, serve, and equip other women in church, business, and executive leadership. I served in this assignment from 2012-2016.

During my tenure as executive director, we developed and designed leadership training events and resources for Women in Leadership and Church

Planting. Our first event attended by over 100 women leaders was called, "Lead like a Woman and Not like a Girl." Another significant ministry we established was hosting the first women in church planting training at the Exponential Church Planters conference in Orlando, Florida. The word "established" in 1 Peter 5:10 speaks of having a settled confidence and commitment to who you are and what God has called you to do. I can testify that if you continue to walk out your "call" to ministry in humility, seeking to be faithful and obedient to the leading of God's Spirit, God will use experiences to help you grow and live out your call with confidence, clarity, and courage. God uses the challenging experiences to grow us in our character, competence, and spiritual maturity, with the goal that we be and look more like Christ.

My next call and invitation to serve in a new ministry context came unexpectedly. In 2016, the bishop of the Florida Conference asked me to serve as a district superintendent, which in our ministry context is an ordained pastor who oversees and administers a region of pastors and congregations. I was asked to serve the largest region with 89 churches over four counties with over twenty thousand members in those congregations. In this season I learned to walk out Matthew 25:23 (NIV), "Well done, good and faithful servant! You have been faithful with a few things; I will put you in charge of many things." I say with great humility, my hope, and prayer is that

God finds us as faithful stewards with God's people, pastors, property, and possessions.

Remember, Sisters, nothing belongs to us, everything belongs to God. God invites us to be stewards in everything. As stewards or people to whom God has given a trust, we must be accountable and responsible. As stewards we will make mistakes and mishandle things. Remember when we "mess up" to always "fess up." Confession, forgiveness, and seeking to make amends for our mistakes in life and ministry is a part of the leadership journey and a part of our Christlike character development and spiritual maturity. I was honored to serve in this ministry assignment for almost five years from 2016 to 2021.

The year 2020 was a game changer for us all. The COVID 19 pandemic and the reckoning of hundreds of years of racial injustice in the public murder of George Floyd caused me to pause and be open to how I could respond to my evolving call to help make the world and my community a more fair, just, and equitable place for everyone. In June 2020, my bishop asked me to lead our conference team in our work of dismantling racism and becoming an anti-racist annual conference as a part of our discipleship strategy. This season invited me to a deeper personal reflection of how I've been shaped, nurtured, and at times harmed, while serving as the first, only, and usually one of few

Black women leading in our predominantly white United Methodist church context. God has been faithful to establish me as a leader who is courageous, confident, and competent and who desires to be faithful to God's calling upon my life for this season of life and ministry.

This time the call and invitation to serve emerged from a new context being higher education and the theological community. I was invited, applied, and was elected to serve as the first female president and dean of the Gammon Theological Seminary, my alma mater. I recently relocated back to Atlanta to start this new ministry appointment. I am still in awe that God brought me back to serve in the same community that significantly shaped and formed me as I answered my call almost twenty-five years ago. I started this new ministry assignment with Gammon Seminary, April 1, 2021, and as of the writing of this book, I've only been in the role for five months. I am in awe of what God has entrusted to my stewardship and care in this season; a school, a staff, and most importantly students who are discerning a call to full-time ministry and desire to be equipped and trained and deployed for such service.

I close with Proverbs 18:16 (ESV), "A man's (woman's) gift makes room for him (her) And brings him (her) before great men (women)." Our God-given gifts, "women", will make room for us and bring us before great people. Our confidence, courage, and competence can grow. Continue to commit to grow and mature in Christ-like character. It's always better to disclose our mistakes instead of hiding them and have them later exposed, yet even when that happens seek forgiveness, make amends, and commit to do better and be better moving forward. Now after being in ministry almost twenty-five years, my desire is "not to have more, do more or be more." I've seen many in ministry who started well but did not finish well. We've seen ministry leaders fall and fail, resign, and be removed from church leadership related to sex, power, and money issues. My prayer is that you trust that God who has begun a good work in you will be faithful to complete it.

QUICK *Tips*

Practical tips for being the only woman at the table:

✓ Communicate clearly and succinctly, bullet points are better. Make it a win-win for as many as possible.

  ✓ You can always have the more detailed report available if it is requested.

✓ Speak up and speak confidently, you are there for a reason.

  ✓ When you don't speak up you are not allowing God to use your voice on that leadership team. Not only will you lose influence there is a likelihood that other women won't get invited to the conversation in the future.

✓ Are women's voices being represented at your church? In your communications, in the classes and events you offer, in your announcements, on stage, etc.

✓ Be aware of what you are wearing—I know, I know, but it's true.

✓ Don't let yourself be the one who sets up the coffee, brings the snacks or even takes the notes. That is not why you are there.

✓ Remember that you are speaking for roughly 60% of your congregation so don't stay silent if you feel an issue is too important.

✓ Lead with your emotions, but don't let your emotions lead you.

✓ Ask if you can bring another female leader with you so that you can continue to invest in and develop other female leaders within the organization.

Chapter 4

YOU ARE MORE THAN JUST: THE PERSON YOU ARE MARRIED TO—BEING MARRIED AND IN THE MINISTRY

Whether you are married, single, divorced, or somewhere in between, it is my hope that this chapter will make you aware of some things you might not have seen coming. I am, by no means, an expert on all things ministry, nor am I an expert on marriage, but I have been in both for over twenty years and it's my prayer that some of the things we discuss in this chapter will be beneficial for you no matter what your current relationship status is.

A quick message for the single female leaders in the ministry

If you are single and in the ministry at the church, then it is my prayer that these words will be beneficial for you one day if you choose to become married. Right now, you are operating in a place that I have personally never experienced, but I have served alongside some incredible female leaders over the years who have been single. You may struggle at times with overwork or get volunteered to do things outside of "office hours" simply because you are single and therefore deemed available, but I would encourage you to prioritize relationships over work. One thing I have consistently heard from friends who are single serving in the ministry is that this was a real challenge for them. Establishing healthy boundaries makes time for healthy relationships in all areas of your life.

There are unique challenges for every woman in ministry whether she is married and in ministry with her spouse, married and her spouse is not in ministry with her, or she is a single woman in the ministry. Find out what works for you in this stage of your life. Ask for help, talk to a mentor or coach, keep open lines of communication within your family and co-workers, and know that you are a valuable asset to the team simply because you are you!

It's my prayer that by learning, reading, and preparing yourself for each season of life and ministry that you will be better equipped and prepared to serve to the best of your ability. The season you are in is exactly where you are supposed to be, so don't rush it or wish it away. Embrace it and watch God move through your faithful obedience. I'm grateful for your grace as you keep reading or even skip over this chapter. Either way, I am so thankful you are here.

For the Pastors' Wives

This chapter is probably geared more for you as a pastor's wife or as someone who is married to someone who works in the ministry. Chances are you either resonate or are bothered by that title. It can be so many things, both spoken by others and unspoken either by others or even yourself, to be in the ministry as a pastor's wife. I've been both a pastor and a pastor's wife and can tell you that neither one is easy, nor is there a "right way" to be when you wear that hat. Ugh, if it were only as easy as wearing a hat. Bing, here's my pastor's wife hat—I'm on. Bing, here's my mom hat—I'm on. Bing, here's my ministry leader hat—I'm on. Bing . . . okay, you get it.

Chances are you wear a lot of other hats and the pastor's wife is just one of them. But let's be honest, it is also one of the most complicated ones that I have ever worn. I don't sing, I don't play the piano, I am not docile nor am I reserved. By all intents and purposes, I don't fit the stereotype of a good pastor's wife. In fact, to say that I do not fit into this ideal would be an understatement. I am a leader who happens to be married to a pastor, which by definition makes me a pastor's wife. This means I am now a target for the enemy, for other women, for other people on staff, and sometimes even for other pastors' wives simply because I do not fit the perceived model of what a pastor's wife should look like, act like, dress like, or anything else that others might think a "good pastor's wife" should behave like on a daily basis. Oh, my goodness, we are a complicated group, aren't we? I would love to say that it is all smooth and easy, but if you've been in the ministry more than five minutes then chances are that you have already experienced the mess that it can be (not always, I promise) to be a pastor's wife.

What I've learned over the years is that pastor's wives (from here on out called PW's) generally get stuck in the cycle of being a PW. It can be a title or role that once it sticks to you it's hard to take it off and be anything other than a PW, but you are way more than that one title. While it is simply one layer of who you are, it's also one that has a lot of unwritten expectations associated with it. I am not just talking about playing the piano, singing on the worship team, or leading the kid's ministry at your church. There's not anything wrong with any of those things, but they can be an expectation that might not necessarily fit within your gifting. Remember, we talked about this in the last chapter—we need to know ourselves, know our gifts, and invest in our leadership.

I tried (and I mean I really tried) to be "Penny Perfect Pastor's Wife" for probably the first five years in the ministry. It was utterly exhausting. At the church I would put on a brave face, pretend to have it all together, then would come home worn out and emotional from being inauthentic to who God created me to be.

He wants more than that for me, and He wants more than that for you as well. You do not have to be "Penny Perfect Pastor's Wife". You are a child of God, and He has uniquely called you and qualified you for ministry, both as a pastor's wife and as your own person. It is completely okay to be you. You can be quirky, strong, confident, shy, introverted, extroverted, and everything in between and that is completely alright. He knew you would be in the position you are in at this point in your life, and He needs *you*, not some made up version of you, to love on, care for, and shepherd those He brings in your path.

Real Ministry Chick Experience

from Frances Chaisson

Lessons learned from life in ministry together

A year after we got married, we felt a restlessness in our souls. We both agreed that God was doing something new and that where we were in life at that moment was just temporary and soon things would change, but there was a lingering question in both of our hearts: "What is it, Lord? What are you asking of us?"

It only took one "what if" conversation between us to open the door for God to start working.

Who knew that God would take just one curious and shaky step from us to "see what happens" as His opportunity to create something greater than we could have ever imagined in ministry, but even greater in our lives?

Eight years working together in ministry have passed by like a whirlwind. We are certainly not marriage experts, nor do we have the most years of experience together in ministry. One thing is sure, we've learned a few lessons along the way—some through tears, others through great joy.

Here are our top four must do's when working in ministry together:

1. Have separate workspaces.

Let's face it, we love our spouse and enjoy hanging out with them, but we all need a healthy amount of personal space. It's healthy for each spouse as an individual and it is healthy for the marriage relationship.

We used to share an office but after the newness wore off, we soon discovered that being in each other's business at all times robbed us from the opportunity to share about our individual ministry experiences at the end of the day.

Since we started working in different offices, I personally enjoy bumping into my husband in the breakroom or just receiving an unexpected visit from him once in a while.

2. Work hard, and rest diligently.

We carry a heavy weight of responsibility working for the Lord and His Church. It may feel as though we must be "on" all the time, ready and available to respond 24/7. This not only places us on a highway to burnout, but it's also not what the Lord wants from us.

Sabbath rest, time alone with the Lord, and the ministry of caring for our families and selves allow us to create healthy boundaries to ensure longevity. Most importantly, when we prioritize rest, we are also trusting God with ourselves and the work we must do.

3. Embrace differences and affirm each other's strengths.

Differences can bring division only when our passion is misplaced to wanting to be right and have our way. Rather, we must intentionally seek to understand each other's point of view, and in humility, affirm and celebrate our partner's strengths as we seek to accomplish the mission together as a team.

It helps to remember that we are one with our spouses and their strengths and accomplishments are ours as well.

4. Make time for fun and friends

Have fun together, do something you both enjoy and create memories. Date nights should be a must, and they do not need to be fancy! Just make it fun and connect with each other.

Also don't shy away from finding time for things that feed you as an individual. Support each other and encourage one another to make space for these things.

Time with friends, mutual and personal, is life giving! Go for the coffee or schedule a double date. Community has a way of revitalizing us, even if you're as introverted as I am. Give it a try and make it intentional.

For women who are leading at the church as a pastor's wife and on staff at the church

Now, let me take a minute to talk specifically to you as a pastor's wife who is also a leader or pastor at the church. I see you. I get you. I am you. I work in the ministry professionally alongside my husband as he leads professionally in the ministry at the local church as well. It's a unique call you have on your life. I've always thought of it more like Priscilla and Aquila, the husband-and-wife tent maker team that served alongside Paul in his ministry for years. They worked together, served together, and were truly connected in all they did. And they were united in their purpose and passion for the local church.

I know this is not the norm and for many years people would joke and say, "Don't you need some time apart from each other?" as if working with your spouse was the weirdest and hardest thing they had ever heard of. While it's not for the faint of heart, it can, and oftentimes does, work well. It takes two very mature people who can work together and with each other both at home and at work. But let me tell you, when it works, it is an amazing sight to see.

When both people are working within their own giftedness, they can learn to rely on the other to fill in the gaps and utilize the other's strengths to maximize their impact. It takes some coordination, scheduling, planning for the family, and decisions about how you are going to act in the office and around the larger church staff. Oh, wait, you mean you have to think through all those details?

Um, yep—you really should. While in some ways you are a couple—on the church staff you are individual team members, each bringing different gifts and skills to complement the team. In whatever meeting, whether within the church staff team or in your congregation, your personal vote (decision) is one vote not two (the assumption is as a couple in the ministry that you are deciding and or voting the same). It took a few years, but we learned to navigate the uncommon path of us both being full time in ministry at the same organization. We often rode separately unless we lived farther than 20 minutes from the church. Then, in a different season, we carpooled because it just made sense to save gas, time, and money at that time.

We worked to make sure that the staff and volunteer teams saw us as individual leaders in our own right. There is nothing more frustrating than to be a strong female leader and people assume you got the job because you are married to the pastor. I know those assumptions happen and I am sure you've experienced them as well, but you know who you are and what you bring to the table, so you don't have to prove you belong there to anyone. Trust me, if you get stuck in that cycle you will have a hard time trying to get out of it, because from that point on everything you do is to show others that you belong there. Let it go. You belong there, God has you there for a reason, and you have nothing to prove—to them or to God. He already knows how awesome you are anyways.

One thing to note: As a pastor's wife who is also on staff as a leader yourself, you will be an anomaly with both groups of women in your world. The other pastors' wives (for the most part, not always) do not work at the church like you do. You have a relationship with them as well as with their spouses because you work together on a daily basis. You will have inside jokes and experiences that they are not a part of. Make it a point to connect with the other pastors' wives regularly. Chances are they might not always understand the dynamics of your relationship with their spouse. Make it known to them how much you love your spouse, how much you love your job, and how grateful you are to work with godly men who love their wives and families so much. You do not want to be perceived as a threat to their marriage or family. It might sound weird and it's tough to even have to say that, but it can be true. If they are not around, they might not fully understand your relationship and work dynamics so being a champion for them is even more important.

It's okay if building these relationships are a little bit extra work. It will be beneficial to you and your ministry if you make these connections a priority. And you would be wise to remember that you don't do this because you must but because there should be healthy respect on all sides of every relationship, and it's better to walk forward together than each one pulling in a different direction.

There's another group of women that you are most likely connected with daily as you work at the church, and that's the other women on the church team. You are one of the girls in the office, but in a lot of ways you are also not "one of the girls" because you are married to one of the pastors on the team. Depending on his position on the team, this could contribute to a great barrier between you and these other women—not because of anything you've done per se, but simply because of who you are married to.

My husband was an executive pastor for the three churches that we've worked at together over the last twenty years. That means that pretty much everyone (myself included) reported to him in the org chart. This can make things tricky. Most of the other women on some of our staff teams were in administrative roles and a few were in leadership roles. I was one of these leaders as a woman on staff, but, in a lot of ways, I was not just "one of the girls" simply because of my role and who my spouse was in the organization. I was married to the second or third in command (depending on the org chart) and that means that 1) I knew a lot of things going on behind the scenes that could not be discussed with others, and 2) all the administrative staff reported directly to him. Like I said, they were mostly women, and they did not always want me around for their lunch time venting and such about their projects and workloads.

I was in their world, but not of their daily world, just as I was a pastor's wife, but generally one of the only pastor's wives that worked full time at the church. I had two groups of women that I wanted to connect with but had different things to worry about and filter through while spending time with each of them. While effort should be made to connect and grow with each group, there will be limitations within each group, which oftentimes left me feeling very isolated and alone.

Real Ministry Chick Experience

from Jessica Bealer

Winning in Marriage and Ministry

I've been in ministry for 20 years. That's a long time, a "full grown adult" amount of time. I know because I have one of those too. My eldest child is a freshman in college this year and like parents often do, I look at him and think, "How did we get here? It feels like we just got started!" It's the same with my ministry. It feels like I blinked, and the years flew by. I guess that's a good thing. If time flies when you're having fun, it means I had some entertaining experiences along the way. I distinctly remember going to Disney World for "research" with my fellow staffers. I recall campus launch Sundays and birthday lunches and tears when interns went off to college. I look back fondly at the hundreds of instances in which I had the opportunity to lead a child to Christ and shouts of celebration as those same children were publicly baptized. I'm even getting a little misty eyed right now as I type these words. I've enjoyed my "job," because it never felt like a burden. It felt like a privilege.

Don't get me wrong—it's not been all fun and games. There were difficult people, passion-lacking seasons, and disastrous situations, but through all the tough times, I had Frank. My husband is both my loudest cheerleader and my ultimate confident. I try to be the same for him. Honestly, I think he does it better. Over the course of our 19 years of marriage, we've seen many different seasons begin and end. There have been times we worked alongside each other, strategizing, executing, and leading within the same ministry. There were also instances in which we were on completely different career paths. Whatever the season, we've made sure our compass always points north. As a couple, it's important for us to understand that God brought us together to navigate this journey called life. However, as individuals we remain aware that our personal calling and assignments may differ. Over the years we've learned how to support each other's goals and career aspirations. With that being said, I want to give you a glimpse of how we make it all work. These four principles have helped to shape our conversations and keep us moving forward.

Pay Attention

There will be times when Frank is going into detail about a project he's working on and while the ins and outs of his daily grind don't always interest me, I force myself to listen intently. The intricacies of his investor call may not be a captivating topic, but if it's important to Frank, then it's important to me. Why? Because the entire highlight reel of my life involves him. I make it a priority to listen, ask questions, and understand so that he can say the reverse is true as well.

Your spouse needs you in his corner, but if you don't even know what's in his corner, that's going to be difficult. Pay attention! Your spouse will thank you.

Promote Your Spouse Publicly

Everyone enjoys a pat on the back, a word of praise, or an accolade to hang on their wall, but when it comes from the person who knows you best it means more. My husband is intimately familiar with my bedhead and my pre-makeup pasty face. He knows my personality flaws, my most embarrassing habits, and my doubts and fears. He knows the undisguised truth about me that I'm so far from perfect and put-together it's ridiculous. So, when the person that knows me best promotes my latest venture or brags about my accomplishments, it means more. If you want to support your spouse's career aspirations, be his biggest fan, his free promoter.

Plan A Party

Celebrate good times, come on! When your spouse wins, you win! This is the "for better" of "for better or worse." Far too often we forget to celebrate the victories of our spouses. I'm not suggesting you have to plan an elaborate bash every time your husband lands an account or gets a promotion or has an amazing breakthrough in the ministry, but there should be a moment of recognition, some way in which you commemorate a job well done. Look for those and plan a party!

Passionately Pursue Jesus Together

I have found the health of my marriage and my spiritual walk are directly linked. When I'm in tune with God, I am a more loving and supportive spouse. Resentment, jealousy, and loneliness find purchase when I take my eyes off our Heavenly Father. If Frank and I want to stay healthy, both as individuals and as a married couple, it all starts with passionately pursuing Jesus together.

I hope these principles will help as you and your spouse grow in love and faith and aspire to go further and do more in your ministry. Achievement is more fun when you have someone to celebrate with.

For the female leader who is leading together with their spouse and leading as an individual

There will be times that you might lead things together with your spouse. There were many times my husband and I co-led classes, Bible studies, training, and such over the years. The reminder here is that in those situations, yes, you are a married couple, but you are also individual leaders helping to equip, train, and prepare those in your church family. Keep it professional, but you can also have fun with it. Yes, he's your husband, but you don't have to hang on his every word and dote on him and neither are you there to "assist" him while he leads the class. Make sure you are still leading while also supporting your spouse.

You want to help in any way you can. That's what leaders do, especially leaders in the Church, but don't diminish yourself to the role of his assistant when you are to be seen as co-leaders. If you do assist in setting up the room or the snacks, make sure he is also assisting in setting up the chairs, or cleaning up afterwards. Little things show that one is not above the other and that you both take your role of leadership as important and yet there are no things that are "too little" for you to do either. It might sound like a thin line, and trust me, it is; yet it is also important for you, for your spouse, and for those that are watching you lead together. It's important for each of you to assert your leadership but also show your servant's heart.

What about those pastors' wives who have been behind the scenes for so long they hesitate to step up and lead with authority? For whatever reason they are shrinking back, hiding their gifts and influence to make others in the church body feel good about their role or to not outshine their spouse. That is a hard and delicate place to be. There's a healthy balance of wanting to be reverent to your spouse and church family, then there's flat out shrinking back. If you have been shrinking back, I want to speak to you for a minute. Stop it. Just stop it. We need you to step up and own your leadership gifts, skills, and abilities. You are not doing anyone any good by being less than all God created you to be.

You don't have to hide to make others feel better, and if you do, maybe that is a good indication that this might not be the best or healthiest fit for you or your family. No, I am not saying you walk all over your church or your spouse. That is not healthy either. But if you are hiding behind his leadership and influence just to keep the peace, you are losing a little bit of yourself each and every day. Take it from someone who did that for a season and not even on purpose. Honestly, I don't think we even realize we are doing it sometimes. I think we get so focused on what's best for "the ministry" that we also forget that we are important as well.

Your spouse can be a fantastic leader, but so can you. He can have incredible gifts that makes him valuable to the leadership of the church or organization, but so can you. You are not there because of your spouse; you are there on your own merits and abilities. The church, ministry, or organization did not hire you because they got a two for one deal (okay, so maybe they did, lol) but now is the time to step up and lead with confidence.

There are women all around you watching to see how you maneuver this season. They need to see strong female leaders who have strong husbands, who both love Jesus but both can stand on their own two feet and lead with confidence. Can you imagine how much better our churches, ministries, and organizations would be if they saw strong male *and* female leaders doing exactly what God created them to do? It would be remarkable. It would be hope filled for everyone in your congregation because they could look around and see "themselves" in you.

It's okay to shine. There is not a biblical mandate that says we are to hide our gifts. On the contrary, it says,

"A city on a hill cannot be hidden (Matthew 5:14)." Don't hide. It can be scary to step up and step out after years of being behind the scenes, but that's what is so awesome about maturity in years and in faith. You can start to settle into who you are, what you bring to the table through your unique wiring, and how it can benefit your church or organization.

There's no one like you. There are other pastors' wives, ministry leaders, and women in ministry, but they are not you. They may have similar passions and even similar skills, but they do not have your unique life experiences that God has allowed in your life so that you could lead at this point. Who knows, you were here for such a time as this (See the book of Esther). If you don't step up and lead like He's created you, He will bring someone else in to do His will. His will *will* be accomplished, but you will miss out on being the chosen vessel He wanted to use to make that happen.

It is a beautiful and wonderful gift to be able to serve in ministry alongside your spouse. It takes some intentional planning, scheduling, and working out all the details together, but it can work, and it can work marvelously, but you have to remember that you are more than just a pastor's wife—you are a leader yourself. Don't forget that when you wear all the different hats that you put on each day.

Real Ministry Chick Experience

from Jaclyn Weidner

When I was a little girl, we had an intercom system through our home phone. Remember home phones? The ones that were bolted to the wall? My little brother would press a button in another room and muffle his voice to sound like God speaking to me. He often said, "Jaclyn . . . this is God . . . go to Africa." He did it partly as a joke to bug me in the way only younger brothers can. But as I've looked back on his joke over the years, I've realized that even then, at that young age, I knew I was made to share the truth of who Jesus is with the world. And in my 10-year-old mind, that meant going to Africa.

Over time I came to realize that I didn't need to go as far as Africa to share about Jesus. As an eighth-grade girl that meant bringing my friends to youth group and even sitting them down on a grassy field one day at lunch to try to explain the Holy Spirit. Seriously, who was that kid? And even though I look back on that particular moment with a slight cringe at my youthful eagerness and boldness, I also kind of love it. I was just living out who I had been created to be. I didn't apologize for it. I didn't hide behind the fear of critical voices or rejection. I just boldly proclaimed the truth to the crowd in front of me. I didn't disqualify myself because I didn't have all the answers to their questions.

I didn't wait for a stage or a platform or count the crowd to see if my message was worth sharing. I was just living out who God had designed me to be by sharing the message He had put on my heart.

But then I got married. And the message of my heart was buried beneath burnout, busyness, and bitterness. My husband became the "one who did ministry," and I raised the kids. And I was fine with that, to be honest. I was so tired. But looking back now, I see that some of the low-lying depression and anxiety I was experiencing came because of me not living out who I was created to be. There were gifts and talents that God had put inside me, but I wasn't using them.

And like so many stories we hear, things got worse before they got better. Postpartum depression with our third had me feeling the worst I had in years. And it was in that place, that deep pit of despair, that I finally turned to face God again. I had been walking with Him, but I wasn't really spending time with Him. Our relationship had taken a back seat to the pressing needs in front of me and it felt routine and forced. It was in that low place where I realized I could not save myself, that He was so near to me. Once again, I began to hear the whisper of His heart in mine and a slow revival began deep within my soul.

He revived the broken, bitter, and barren places and put a new fire in my heart. I was a new woman, and yet, I was still that same little girl who desired to share the love of Jesus with those all around her. And as I live out the call of God on my life using the gifts, He has placed inside of me, I am continually revived. It is when I back down and let the voice of the enemy try to silence me or lie to me, saying that it is better for me to lay low, that a sort of heaviness and low-lying anxiety seems to set in.

I began to realize that I was made to shine! And I know that can sound a little bold to say, but it's true. Jesus lives inside of me, and His light is meant to be on display! "Let your light shine before others" (Matthew 5:16 NIV). And of course, there are times where I make it all about me! Can I be honest and share that this is a confusing time to do "ministry." We measure in numbers and applause, and it's easy to let our obedience and surrender turn to striving and performance. I don't think there is a single woman in ministry that hasn't struggled with this at some point. And I don't know what works for everyone, but I will tell you what has helped me throw off the fear of what others think, and the misplaced worship of myself. It is daily time with the One who continues to refine me, getting quiet and really listening, asking Him to search my heart (Psalm 139:23-24), and confessing and repenting daily.

It is in that quiet place that I know where I am off course, and He gently invites me back on the right path. And it's in this quiet place where He gives me guidance for the next leg of the race and my confidence in my calling grows. I didn't call myself! I didn't give myself these desires and these gifts and talents. He did! And He fully expects me to use them and grow them! And with a humble heart posture to first know Him, and surrender it all to Him, that is the place where I am able to fully run the race, He has called me to. I come alive when I am doing the thing I was created for. There is nothing quite like it.

For the female leaders who lead at the church whose spouse works outside of the ministry

What about being married while in the ministry and your spouse does not work at the church? This is something that I see quite often, and it is always very exciting. Mostly because for over twenty years this was outside of what I have personally experienced, but things have recently changed, and it is something I am experiencing now. It takes a lot of work to be in the ministry. It also takes a lot of work to have a good marriage, right? So, it all comes down to communication. You love your job (the world might call it a job, but for those in the ministry we know that it is a calling; a job would be way easier than what you are do- ing) and you love your spouse, obviously, or you wouldn't be married.

Since I started writing this book this has been my new reality. After more than 20 years in the ministry together my husband now has a marketplace job, and I am still in the ministry at the local church. This means our schedules are completely out of sync for the first time in over two decades. It has been a struggle to create a rhythm that works for us to stay connected and involved in each other's lives, but it is a good struggle because it means we are working on it. We have not perfected it by any means, but we are continuing (it's only been six months now) to tweak, adjust, and see what works.

It is important to sit down together and find out a rhythm that works for your family. They might work Monday through Friday 9-5 and you probably work Monday through Thursday and maybe the weekends too. How do you juggle the demands of ministry and marriage? Through intentional and thought-out planning. You are going to want to look at the calendar and mark the date day or night in there. That is a priority. You also should consider when you will go to church together and actually sit together. Someone literally just laughed out loud while reading that because for the longest time we never went to church together as a family, much less as a couple.

Whatever it takes, you need to try to figure that out and make it happen. If you work on the weekend there is a high likelihood that you are distracted and all over the place. I get it! I was there too. But it is incredibly important for your marriage, specifically to your spouse, for you to be able to go to church and sit together . . . especially if he is not on staff like you are. He is not in the day-to-day stuff going on behind the scenes and church is something different for him than it is for you. Yes, he knows what you tell him about what is going on, but he is not in the thick of it day in and day out and that's okay. He can give you a fresh perspective on things without being in the thick of it, which is why I believe that it is incredibly important for you to worship and attend church together for at least one service each weekend.

Chick **CHAT**

Real, practical advice on being a female leader in the ministry to lead well while balancing your marriage and/or leading together while still being your own leader.

> *Married to someone on church staff. (We actually have quite a few married couples on our staff.) My husband and I planted a church 16 years ago. He is lead pastor; I am Multi-Site Director. I always tell married couples to know what hat you are wearing in conversations with one another and announce it. We struggled with this at first, but once we started identifying the role, we were in at that moment it helped to clarify. Simple statements like, "This is your wife speaking here," or "As the Multi-Site Director . . . " – Christie*

> *Married while I was a staff pastor, and he had a secular job. The reason why we were able to balance life well was because we were super supportive of*

each other. There was no jealously on either side. We knew each other's calling and pushed each other in that direction. – Rachael

This is me! I'm married and my husband and I are both on full time staff at the church. He is the Worship and Creative Arts pastor, and I am the Kids Ministry Director. Our situation is unique in that I am on the management team (senior staff team) and he is not. Communicate, communicate, communicate. Communicate schedules, trips, and busy seasons. There will be slack to pick up during each person's busy season. Identifying this early and having a plan is crucial, especially if you have kids. Have a clear understanding of confidentiality and how that could affect your ability to share things with your spouse. Thoroughly discuss expectations for interacting at a personal and professional level—in meetings (i.e., how to handle disagreements as you advocate for your ministry), PDA (public displays of affection) during workday, and leadership hierarchy (this can be very damaging if not dealt with properly—i.e., spouses should not be in a direct line of supervision of each other.) – Marlena

I'm a married pastor and my husband is not in ministry. Consider how every "yes" in ministry will impact your marriage . . . time, energy, etc. I made vows to my husband that I need to honor regardless of my ministry role . . . ministry is not a reason to neglect them or put my marriage behind the needs (more accurately the wants) of the church. – Jen

We are both on staff. Our motto "never sacrifice your family on the altar of ministry." God first, family second, ministry third. Also maintaining an amazing health marriage, we get away once a quarter, even for one night, just to be a couple, not parents or pastors. – Tara

Put firm boundaries on your time. Don't be more available to those you minister to than you are to your spouse. Develop the spiritual discipline of observing a sabbath, in which you disconnect from responsibilities to your church or ministry. – Jaimme

We are married, have children, and are both on staff (in New Zealand). Always family comes first— unless it's an emergency. Make your days off your days off. Create a culture with your staff that unless it's an emergency they don't contact you on days off. Tell them to write the message down so they don't forget and can get it out of their mind so you can enjoy your day off. Let the congregation know when it's staff's days off and who to contact in an emergency. Qualify what is considered an emergency. Make time for yourselves as a couple and as individuals. Try not to talk about work at home (not always easy) and phones off during dinner time. If you teach people that your time is just as precious as theirs, they will learn to appreciate you and what you do, rather than take you for granted and expect that you be at their beckon call. – Pip

Pick a night of the week you'll both be home and protect it for time together. The night might change depending on the season but it's an easy no when you have a standing block on your calendar and it's an easy yes to your marriage. I was the one on church staff. – Dianne

My husband is an Army chaplain, and I am working to become a military reserve chaplain myself, which doesn't happen very often in my circles at all. Your spouse's calling is not your identity, nor the identity of your family. If the ministry spouse's career is more demanding, don't center your entire schedule around their schedule and its demands. Maintain a sense of what you need and stick to it even as you accommodate your life for them. Not every expectation people put on you as a ministry spouse is a standard you need to live up to. Don't shrink, especially as a woman. Take up space, even if your husband is in ministry, too. You are not less credible. You have the authority of Christ and the Spirit, too, so use your voice as you are able with true and humble confidence. – Aria

QUICK *Tips*

Practical tips for you as a female leader while your spouse serves in ministry.

✓ You are a leader in and of yourself, and so is your spouse. Support him, encourage him, and be his biggest encouragement. There are plenty of other people that will tear him down, don't let one of them be you. Yes, speak the truth in love, but have his back. He needs that more than you might know.

✓ Pray for your spouse. You know what he deals with daily, but there are probably things going on of which you don't know the full details. That is hard to swallow when you hope and pray for a no-secrets marriage, but the reality is, depending on where they fall in the org chart, they might be privy to information of which you should not have access. It's hard but be okay with that because more often than not, you really don't want to know anyways.

✓ Get to know some of the other staff or pastors' wives on the team. Nurture a supportive friendship with them and let them know that you are praying for their family as they serve in your church family.

Practical tips for you as a female leader as you serve in ministry with your spouse.

✓ Be for each other, but don't defend each other in meetings.

✓ Be your own person, come into meetings on your own, not together.

✓ If you can, drive to the office on your own, as well as make lunch/coffee meetings without your spouse present. You are not a duo. You are your own leader with your own teams.

✓ Don't be defensive if someone on staff says something that you don't agree with about your spouse or their decision on a topic.

✓ Lead with your giftedness as we talked about it in depth in a previous chapter. If your gifts aren't behind the scenes, then get out there and do what God created you to do. Let this also be your guide as you lead with your spouse at the church.

✓ Consider having a Christian counselor in your corner. This is even more important for you as a leader, but also as a married couple in the ministry.

Practical tips to stepping into your leadership after years of being behind the scenes.

✓ Talk to your spouse and let them know that you feel God nudging you to step up and lead at a higher level. Let them know that things are going to look a little different and maybe share some of the ideas discussed earlier in the book.

✓ Pray and ask God for boldness and a holy confidence to step out and lead like He's been leading you to do. He will be there every step of the way with you.

✓ Start making sure you are leading in and of your own self. This may mean that your spouse will need to get someone else to help them set up for a class or prep for a group, and that's okay. There are plenty of people that are waiting to be asked to serve.

✓ Find ways you can start to lead, whether it is a Bible study with some of the other pastors' wives, a class on the weekend, or in a discipleship group. Look for ways to lead that fit within your giftedness and the church's needs.

✓ Listen, learn, and watch for opportunities to make a difference wherever God places you. Chances are you are already doing this, but intentionally seeking new ways always brings fresh eyes to each situation.

✓ Ask a friend or other female leader to be an accountability partner for you as you seek to step out of your comfort zone.

✓ Seek a Christian life coach who can help you set goals and start making progress in breaking through this behind-the-scenes barrier in your life. (Trust me on this one. It is worth it. The biggest areas of growth for me have always happened after spending time with a trusted ministry coach.)

Chapter 5

YOU ARE MORE THAN JUST: THE PEOPLE YOU ARE RAISING— BEING A MOM IN MINISTRY

If you are a mom and you are in the ministry things are just a little more complicated for you. The struggle is real, the demands are real, and the balance of the two is never-ending. My hope in addressing motherhood and the ministry is two-fold. First, if you are a mom who is in the ministry, I pray that it brings you hope and practical ideas on balancing both. Second, if you are not a mom yet, but you are a woman in the ministry, maybe this will open your eyes to some of the other needs and demands of the other women whom you lead or serve with as well as prepare you to one day be a mom in the ministry (if that is ahead for you). Either way, if this is you, keep reading, my friend.

There are different seasons of motherhood and ministry. It can be equally challenging to live within your giftedness and calling while you embrace the roles that God has called you to at that time, whether it is as an aunt, godmother, friend, or even as a parent through adoption, fostering, or birth. And there are not only different seasons of mother-hood, but there are also different ways to get to that role with some struggling with infertility and longing to wear the badge of motherhood.

Wherever you find yourself as you read this, please know this, you are right where God wants you to be. I know that's not always easy to hear, whether you want to be a mom more than anything and still are not, or if you are buried under a pile of laundry wondering if you are ever going to have a day when it feels like you made ac-complished all you set out to do.

It's complicated, and as a woman who is going to find her community, own her leadership, and take the next step this is one space where it might feel as if you might never measure up. Yep, I get it. Here's the thing, pretty much every other woman alive gets it too. You might not see it on her Instagram feed or perfectly planned out stories, but we all can struggle with feeling "less than" when it comes to this part of our life.

And while all that is true, motherhood (in whatever way it looks like in your world) *is* a very special and high calling. There's nothing like it. You can feel like Wonder Woman one moment and like the gum on the bottom of some-one's shoe the next. Talk about humbling!

But there's a delicate balance one must strike as a woman who leads in ministry and has a family at home. Whether your spouse is in the ministry or works outside of the church, you have extra hats you wear that are made just for you. There is no one else that was picked to be the mom of your children. People will always tell you that it flies by in the blink of an eye and truthfully when you are neck deep in it you think those people are looney because each day feels like a year. But hold on tight, dear friend! This too shall pass and there will come a time when you look around and miss the chaos, even if it's just a little bit.

When you are in the ministry while also raising kids at home, there is a constant tug of war between your calling and your family that silently happens in the depths of your soul. I would love to just take a minute to talk about this because as a mama who has been there and done that, I can tell you from experience that the wrestling is very real, and there is only one person that God called to be the mama to your kids—you.

Motherhood in ministry can be tricky, but it can also absolutely work. Just like everything else, though, it takes strategic work, planning, and a lot of flexibility. I used to tell people all the time that you must be a little like Gumby to be a mom leading in ministry. You will bend and flex and twist, and when it feels like you might break you straighten back out again and then voila! Things are okay.

Is that true all the time? No, that would be naive to believe, but it can be true if you work together as a family and figure out what your non-negotiables are—for you, for your spouse, and for your family. What we think may be most important may not be so after discussion, and they will likely change depending on the age and stage of your children. What I can tell you is this—your family is your *first* ministry. They are the very first thing God has called you to lead and love well. It does not matter how big, mighty, and influential your other ministry(ies) is if you are not leading your family well. As I mentioned earlier, I have wrestled with this.

When I felt the call to ministry, my kids were nine and seven years of age. I knew there were a few non-negotiables for us, and one of them was that I would drive my kids to and from school each day. This was prime time for them to chat and share about their day, so I was not willing to give up that time with them. When the church approached me about a job, I already knew I needed to have this drive time built into my schedule. I brought it to the attention of my supervisor early in the contract discussion and it was easy for them to agree that I would be offline and off campus during those times.

There are also seasons in motherhood when you are needed more and those in which your children are more independent. Look for and be aware of those seasons in your motherhood and pray to determine the needs of your family during these seasons. There really is no right or wrong answer. Trust me though, there will be people who think they have the answer—and they might for their family, but that does not mean it is right for your family.

This is where it is so important to be grounded in your own personal faith walk so you can discern what God is trying to tell you in each of these seasons. If you've been a mom for more than a minute, then you know that each day is just a little different than the day before. Your children are learning new things at an exponential rate, so what works today might not work tomorrow. This is why it is even more important to be flexible in your expectations of yourself, of the ministry, and of your family.

Real Ministry Chick Experience

from Jaclyn Weidner

24 years ago, I attended my very first Young Life event. It was hosted at my future husband's house. How's that for a divine appointment? Nine years later, after we both spent time on staff, we married. I jumped right in as a volunteer leader and committee member. My husband was on full-time staff, and I taught at the local high school. Our entire world revolved around ministry to high school students. Our boundaries were non-existent, so investing in our marriage looked like lounging on the couch recovering from whatever late-night adventure we had drummed up the night before.

It didn't take long for burnout and bitterness to become the fruit from our lack of ministry boundaries.

Fast forward another 5 years and we had our first daughter. We knew something had to change but we really didn't know how to do it. Foot on the gas had been our mode of operation for so long and we feared that if we stepped back at all, things in our ministry would fall apart.

By baby number 3, things were falling apart. But not in the ministry. I was diagnosed with postpartum

111

depression, and this was the wakeup call we needed. It was a slow road with having to un-learn how ministry had been done previously. For my husband, it was learning to let go of being in the "know" in every decision, the "go-to" person for all troubleshooting and issues and learning to trust others in the organization. He also learned to create boundaries with his work schedule. He started limiting the nights out a week and weekend trips, learning to say no even if it meant disappointing others. For my part, I had to confess my anger, my bitterness towards my husband and his work, and this was what ultimately led to my healing, from not only postpartum depression but my low-lying depression and anxiety.

We learned to prioritize rest, blocking out a weekly sabbath, and creating rhythms for our family to connect. As our kids got a little older and we had implemented these healthier boundaries and rhythms into our schedule, we learned to seek out ways to include our family in ministry. We knew isolation wasn't the answer; it was firm boundaries that were needed, and eventually we regained the desire to be more inclusive. Our kids love it when meetings are held in our home with the "big kids," or when they get to see Dad at work during a larger event.

Sometimes the ministry desires God puts on our hearts feel so strong we want to make them happen at any cost. I believe God wants to do incredible things through us, but not at the cost of our health and family relationship. Rather, we need to trust Him and partner with Him knowing He is the one that will bear the fruit we desire. We simply get to work alongside Him in it.

Can I share with you from a very transparent and heartfelt place for a minute? There might come a time when the ministry is so intense, so active, and so busy that you can feel the tug and pull on your family, but you continue to plow ahead because it's the church and they need you. You might be tempted to think your family will understand because they know how important the ministry is to you—and they do—but please do not sacrifice your family on the altar of ministry.

Do not let your ministry, your role, or your church become an idol of the most important thing in your life. Oh, I know, we think it won't happen to us, but chances are if you are a driven leader, a go-get-it-done kind of girl, then you are going to wrestle with this a time or two in your ministry career. And when you do, I hope that you remember this sentence. Don't sacrifice your family on the altar of ministry.

Your family is your very first ministry and you only get one family and one chance with that family. Every day, your family is watching to see who or what is more of a priority in your life—the church or them. Yes, I know, that sounds harsh and maybe a little heavy as well, but as someone that has seen the fallout of those intense ministry seasons in my own family, I can tell you this, it is much better to be proactive instead of reactive. If you plan and prepare ahead of time for the intense ministry seasons, then you are better prepared to deal with it. If an issue comes from left field and you are unprepared for it, it can take you down or put you on the sidelines for a bit.

This is a lesson that I learned the hard way. After years and years of driving hard and fast for the ministry, I saw the effects (too late) that it unintentionally had on my family. Now that my kids are adults, we are still repairing some of the damage from those intense ministry seasons. God is so good, and He can do anything, and yes, He can make it all work out, but if we are intentionally caring for, shepherding, and prioritizing our family, then we don't have to wait until things get way off course to fix them. We can catch it while it's happening.

Special note, if you and your husband are both in the ministry, then you know that extra pressure is put on your kids—not only as a staff kid, but now as a pastor's kid. At each age and stage of your child's life there will be unwritten expectations for them, whether they are expected to be the personification of perfection, knowing Scriptures better and faster than others, being flexible when they are "stuck" at church yet again, or even when someone from the church interrupts their family time . . . again. I would love to say that this is no longer the case, but I think we both know that it still is. Hopefully there will come a time when our kids, as staff and pastoral kids, can simply be themselves, but until others can set down those expectations and see our kids as simply kids, it is important that we do that as much as we can for them. They do not have to be perfect; they don't have to know the most Scripture, all the books of the Bible by the time they are three or play every instrument in the student band. We, as their parents, can give them the space and grace they need to figure out who they are in Christ while we plant the seeds of God's love (1 Corinthians 3:6) into their hearts.

You, dear friend, are more than just the people you are raising. You are a mom, and you are a leader, so you certainly wear many hats, but it's important to remember you are a child of God first. If we can start to develop that same understanding into our own kids' lives early on, how much better would their lives be as they get older?

To have a rich and deep grounding in who God made them to be while also developing their own God given gifts and skills is a sweet and beautiful gift we can give to our child(ren). We first have to settle on who we are and live it out each day in front of them. We know they are watching. Because of this, we must determine whether how we live, how we work, how we talk, and what we do each day communicates the right things.

Let's talk about some ways we create a healthy and positive way to integrate our kids into our ministries and still let them be kids.

» Look at the age and stage of your child right now, as well as the love language of your child (see *The Five Love Languages* by Townsend and Cloud). Intentionally invest in expressing love to your child in the way they receive love.

» Plan ahead for weekends with lots of services, staff retreats, and holidays. How can you make sure to be present and involved while also living out your calling?

  » What are some ways that you can still make the holidays special for your kids?

» Talk to someone in the ministry who has kids at the stage right after your kid's age/stage of life. Ask them what worked, what didn't work, and what they wish they had known at the time.

  » Then share that insight with others at the same life and age stage as your family.

» Be willing to be flexible but also firm. If there is a specific family event you need to attend, find someone to cover for you at work so you can be fully present with your family when you need to be.

» Ask your senior leadership to invest in a staff kids' space where the staff/ministry/pastor's kids can have a reprieve. This should be a safe place just for them. This is especially important if there are multiple services each weekend.

  » In that same space, hire a childcare team to cover this space. It's important that it is a safe space, but also a protected space. Like it or not, your kids can become a target to people who don't always have the best intentions. Just because you "work" at a church does not mean it is a "safe" place. The lost, lonely, and broken attend your church; and while we don't look at everyone as troublesome, it is always better to be safe than sorry.

» Listen to your kids. I know, I know, they can have lots of opinions and lots of things to say about this, that, and the other, but really lean in and listen to their ideas, suggestions, and concerns about either attending so many services or even the people with whom you serve and lead. You would be surprised at just how intuitive kids can really be.

Real Ministry Chick Experience
from Toni Nieuwhof

When Carey, my husband, and I were raising our two sons, we (probably like you!) had full lives. Carey and I met in law school, and then he went to seminary while I practiced my pre-law profession as a pharmacist.

While Carey was still in seminary, he was offered a couple of lucrative positions in Toronto. We've only had clear visions from God a handful of times, but one of them was shared, and it was based on Paul's story of the man who said, "Come over to Macedonia and help us!" (Acts 16:9 NIV) We both saw the then-moderator admonishing us with those same words.

The churches we were called to were willing, eager, and relatively wealth poor. God provided a lovely, experienced woman, Sue, to care for our infant and preschooler so I could work part-time to help us pay the bills.

Over many of those years, I finished off my qualifications as a lawyer and then worked in various leadership roles in our local hospitals. Carey was the senior pastor of our church. Our boys studied music and loved sports like hockey and baseball, so our calendars involved many moving parts. We needed help.

Sue was a vital part of our lives. Although the kids' needs always came first, she also helped out with laundry and cleaning. (She would also smuggle hot dogs for my younger son, which no one told me for years!) Our kids love her to this day.

There were others who helped make the calendar happen. We hired stuff out. Carey jokes that he has a guy for everything. We developed friendships with other parents and could carpool or ask for favours when we had schedule conflicts.

These measures facilitated a saner life, but on their own, they wouldn't have gone far enough. Carey and I worked closely together to ensure, as much as we could, that at least one of us would be home during the afterschool period from about 4–8 pm. That meant for a season of years, Carey left the church at 3:30 pm. Our work cultures at that time centered on a 9–5 pm day, so he sometimes needed to be assertive when people tried to grab his attention as he was heading out.

I realize that it's far more common for schedules to be fitted around the needs of those who are producing the outcomes, especially after the pandemic, but one of the causes of marriage breakups over this last year has been resentment over inequitable sharing of domestic responsibilities. Are the two of you shouldering similar loads at home? Are there adjustments that need to be made for the sake of peace for everyone? Are there tasks that you need to pay someone outside your family to do for you two? Yes, that may require a financial sacrifice for a season, but think of it as a relational investment.

All of this to say—my hope and prayer for your marriage and family is that you'll waste no time addressing the rough parts at home and live in the energy and peace God so desires for you!

Chick CHAT

Real, practical advice on being a female leader in the ministry and creative ways to include your kids in the ministry:

Decide in advance, that as far as it is possible, you will do ministry in a way that allows your children to always love the church. – Kyla

I am a full-time staff member in A/V ministry, so it's not always easy for my 3.5-year-old son to help me. But he can help me carry things (tape, small boxes, short cables) and he can hold doors. He is also great at pushing the elevator buttons. Today, he helped me by mopping our stage floor. He is also a fantastic helper with moving and stacking Operation Christmas Child shoe boxes. Serving is a normal part of my life and I am making it a normal part of his. – April

My daughter is now taking piano and voice lessons so that when I travel to preach, she can be my musician. My son will also take dance classes so they can both dance as well. They are on the youth dance team at church. They also help me in any hospitality ministry that needs to be done. – Shakema

You are never too young to serve and be made to feel you are an important part of the team. We took our boys, 12 months and 3-years-old, to hand out Easter egg bags at our church drive through. We all worked with my 3-year-old to let him pass out as many as he wanted. Sure, it took a little longer and we had to lift him a lot so he could reach, but he helped.

— Samantha

We started with preparing a delivering food to people/leaders they see at church. We baked cookies and cake, cooked lots of things made in our big gumbo pot (soup, gumbo, chicken potpie), and baked fresh bread (we had started this whenever we moved into a new home for every neighbor, one at a time). As they moved into upper elementary and middle school, they played drums and piano for the little-littles and Sunday night services and started picking out who to deliver food to once a month or so. When in high school, our daughter and I asked if we could lead a summer Sunday school class for girls in 4th-6th grade and invited other mother-daughter teams to co-lead with us so I could grow intergenerational relationships between my high schooler and the other women in our church. Both our son and daughter are full-on active members of their own local churches and never missed a beat, even in college. Those relationships with other godly men and women gave them deeper connections to the family of faith. — DeDe

Babywear infants. As they've gotten older, we talk about what I'm up to and why I'm going up to church. When they ask, "Why do you talk to so many

people?" I tell them it's because God loves people and I want them to feel loved. – Dianne

Invite your kids into an understanding of confidentiality early. In a ministry home, kids hear things so you have to talk early with them about how information can make us feel special, but that in our home we are careful only to share our own stories. Then be sure to honor this rule yourself being cautious not to share stories about your children without seeking their consent in advance. – Kyla

Cultivate a servant's heart toward others by praying with your kids for those who are shut in or sick. Then ask them what ideas they have on ways they can be a blessing to that person. With our daughters they made cards or helped with baking a treat then we would deliver. Their reward was instant when they could see how blessed others were for their prayers and giving. The girls would also be able to see answers to their prayers, increasing their own faith and encouraging them to pray even more. – Yvonne

We tried to balance things so that our kids didn't feel like they had to be at church all the time or were always helping us out with ministry. I guess we picked and chose what things we were already doing that they might have fun helping with. Our kids are now 18 and 20 and they are involved in their own churches because they chose on their own to seek out a healthy church where God put them. The marriage ministry at our church put on a BBQ after service one Sunday, and we invited our kids to participate by handing out hamburgers. We tried to ask as much as possible if they would like to help with something, like childcare, instead of just telling them they would be helping for convenience.

If there was a time we were away and they were with friends or relatives, we thanked them for investing in the kingdom by being okay with Mom and Dad being away that night. We shared with them confidentially the praises of what God was doing in couples. We also got to be part of a local volunteer group through Family Life that had an annual retreat/camping trip with kids included, and they included the kids in leading worship. This was huge because the kids were poured into by other adults in the same type of ministry, which made them feel valued, cared for, and connected to other kids that had parents doing the same thing. – Kim

I have taken my toddler along to deliver care packages to people I minister to who are sick. (This happened a lot with COVID!) He was excited to be a part of the surprises and I think this small way of including him in ministry which taught him to think of others' needs.

– Amanda

I have always served in ministry where I could include my kids in most of what I did. Greeting, children's ministry, meals ministry, etc. – Sabrina

My kids will tell anyone, and at times with a slight eye roll lol, Mama says, "You see the vision, you get the job." Simply put, if you see a need or task, you can fulfill it. It means you have the solution. We speak about how in a world of me, me, me . . . it's a rare gift to notice others, but it's what we've been empowered and challenged to do. With my younger two, ages 15 and 12, I am much better at understanding their personal giftings and how they can contribute based on them. It's a wonder to watch how their giftings and service flow together and the contentment that comes from it. We also allow them to say no or not now so they are never treated as if it is their sole job to serve others, but rather, what they contribute is part of the whole. Better together. Stronger together. – Brenda

We help our kids be a part by giving them three things. We give them a task (or they pick which parent to help.) We help them understand why we are doing this task. We help them see how blessed they are by serving. Making going to church fun is super important when we are there a lot! – Stephanie

QUICK *Tips*

Let's get practical when we talk about our ministry and being a mom. What are some things you can do to balance the two?

✓ Root your own personal identity deep in Christ so you do not bend under the pressure of ministry and motherhood.

✓ Realize that each age and stage of your children's lives is going to be different with unique needs. Stay alert and aware of those changes. This will help you be proactive instead of reactive in your parenting.

✓ Allow your kids to be kids. Whether they are staff kids or pastor's kids, they need to see the church as a safe place where they can be themselves.

✓ Don't sacrifice your family on the altar of ministry—what does that practically look like in your life and ministry?

✓ In each season of ministry proactively seek out family time so that it doesn't slide by with all the busyness of the ministry.

Section Two

YOU WERE MADE
FOR MORE

How to Move Forward
in Your Leadership
Development

Chapter 6

YOU WERE MADE FOR MORE: IT'S TIME TO FIND YOUR COMMUNITY

You were made for more. Don't get me wrong. I believe with my whole heart that you are probably out there killing it right now. You are doing hard work. We all go through seasons and circumstances that make ministry more challenging than others. The COVID pandemic we have been experiencing globally over the last two years is a great example of the kind of challenge I'm talking about. Ministry looks completely different than it ever has and yet we need you now more than ever. The funny thing about ministry is that too often we can get so focused on getting it done that we often go at it alone.

Yes, there are people around us, and yes, we probably have teams we work with, but I'm talking about feeling alone—and that loneliness is pervading our society right now. We are more connected than ever and yet, statistically, more people are dealing with epidemic levels of loneliness and depression. In an article by ACSTechnologies in December 2021 it was said that "loneliness continues to rise and our ability to make lasting connections seems to be more and more difficult. Individuals who listed "making friends/loneliness" as an escalating concern increased 40% from 2017-2021 (23.1 million Americans) and people who listed "making friends/loneliness" as a high concern increased 100% from 2017-2021 (19.8 million Americans)."[7] How can that be when the world feels more connected than ever? I am not a scientist, and I certainly don't have all the answers on this topic, but what I do know is this—we were not made to do life (or ministry) alone.

Some of you might argue that you can get more done that way, which might be true for some of you, but it is critically important for us to find our community. And when I say 'community,' I'm talking about finding your people. These are people that get you and have your back. My definition of community is a safe place with your people, the ones that you can authentically be around without having to be "on" all the time.

As a woman in ministry, you are likely more than aware that you are always on, always being watched, and always need to be careful of what you say, both in person and online. I cannot even begin to tell you how many times I have looked around a restaurant, coffee shop, or wherever I am before I say something just to make sure that it wasn't going to be overheard. And this is not because anything I was sharing was bad or derogatory, but simply because I know that in my world (okay, so most of the world right now) I know how easy it is to misunderstand something when it's taken out of context or when those listening don't have the benefit of the entire story, or your intentions.

It can be exhausting just to be a woman in the ministry, but to be a woman in the ministry that is always on and always wearing one of many hats can flat out wear you out. Trying to be everything to everyone is exhausting. What do you do? How do you make sure to be careful and aware all the time as well? This is where it comes back to your community once again.

It's so easy for us to get lost in our thoughts. Imposter syndrome is when the spiral starts of doubting who we are, what we bring to the table, the gifts we have, and why we are even doing what we are doing. If you don't have a strong community of people in your corner, it can be confusing at times and downright lonely at other times. And here's the thing with loneliness, it is growing at epidemic proportions and when it "looks" like we are more connected than ever, the reality is that we are lonelier than ever.

In May 2018 there was a study done by Cigna, a global health service company, revealing that loneliness is at epidemic levels in America. In the study it cited that only around half of Americans (53 percent) have meaningful in-person social interactions, such as having an extended conversation with a friend or spending quality time with family, on a daily basis.[8] Cigna also found that Generation Z is the loneliest generation and claims to be in worse health than older generations.[9] In October 2020 in an online article posted by the Barna Group it said, "In research conducted for *The Connected Generation*, Barna's largest-ever study, data show that half of U.S. 18–35-year-olds (49%) expressed anxiety over important decisions and were afraid to fail. Over three in 10 said they often felt sad or depressed (39%) or lonely and isolated from others (34%)."[10] That was just a few years ago. I cannot even begin to imagine what the statistics would be today. (While I am writing this we are in a season of a global pandemic.)

Let's face it, leadership can oftentimes be lonely, but it doesn't have to be that way. No matter if we are in ministry, the marketplace, or even at home, we don't have to buy into the lie that it's just the way it is, and all leaders feel that way.

It's my hope that by digging in on this discussion, I can help you see that with some practical ideas we can carefully cultivate a rhythm of connection into our lives so that we can lead from a healthy place. What exactly does the word "connection" mean? I like to deal with facts, so I went straight to dictionary.com and did a little research on this and here's what I found. Connection is:

» The act or state of connecting, or even, the state of being connected.

» It was also an association or relationship.

» A circle of friends or associates or a member of such a circle. (This is my favorite.)

As stated earlier, I've been on staff at the local church for more than 20 years and in that time I did just about every job you can do; and on top of that I was not only a pastor or ministry leader, but also a pastor's wife. See, I told you ministry can make authentic connection complicated! For so many years it "looked" like I had a lot of friends and yet the reality was that I had a lot of "friends" but not very many deeply meaningful gut-level honest friends in my life.

As a woman in a professional ministry, as a pastor, pastor's wife, ministry leader, or whatever hat I was wearing, I was keenly aware that I needed to be on guard. This made me feel isolated from, lonely for, and misunderstood by others. And it coerced me to walk through the fire with only my family because it just never felt "safe" to be the real me outside my home. I had lots of friendships that were miles wide, but never more than an inch deep. You know, surface-only type relationships. I didn't allow friends to get too close so I could protect myself, the ministry, my family, the church, you name it, but mostly because of my leadership position. And yes, you do have to be aware of and careful to find "safe" people in your life with whom you can be fully you, while also protecting those you lead or the leadership position you are in.

If you would allow me a minute to be extra transparent with you, the big shift happened for me when our oldest son was in the hospital, and we ended up being there for 51 days. In that time, life was completely out of control, and I had no other option but to lean into whatever God was doing, and I saw Him move in the most amazing and unexpected ways. Every day for those 51 days in the hospital we never missed a day when one, sometimes two, meals were brought to us.

At one point the security guard came to our room and said, "Who are you people?" Simple question, but what was really happening was the power of community. God showed me at that time that I didn't have to "have it all together" or be "a perfect pastor's wife", I simply needed to be me and love those that God put around me.

After that horrible season finally came to a close (our oldest son is now a healthy, strong godly adult man with his own family now—thank you Jesus), I started to shed other people's expectations and simply lean into what God was asking me to do each day. It was not an easy season, both during it and even afterwards for a while, but God (again, my two favorite words when paired together) was preparing me, as well as my ministry, for a brand-new adventure of faith as well as the revelation of the importance of finding your community.

I'd love to take some time today to share with you what I've learned over the years about finding your community. To keep from being isolated and to step into the fullness of who God created you to be, I believe that there are three main lanes when it comes to deepening your connections. They are community with God, community with family, and community with friends. In my opinion there is a proper order to these connections within our community and when that order is done well, they stack upon each other and allow us the best opportunity to live our best life.

Community with God

I would love to take you through a little visual of how I like to see each of our communities. I like to think of it as a cupcake—a beautifully decorated and absolutely yummy cupcake. Are you picturing it yet? You know, the cupcake that is almost too perfect to eat, but let's face it, you are going to eat it anyways. It is robust, full of that glorious buttercream icing, and topped with the most magnificent sprinkles that you've ever seen. Anyone else need to stop and go get a cupcake right now? No? Me either. This cupcake represents our community. It is in a specific order when it is made for a reason, not the ingredients, but in the presentation, because you start with the cupcake and build up. If it is not built up in the specific order of cupcake first, then icing, then add in some sprinkles, then it is simply smooshed and while it still might taste as good it certainly just doesn't feel right nor does it have that same beauty to it. That's how I see the three layers of community. We need to be healthy, strong, and whole as children of God first, but also as female leaders in the church.

The base is the foundation that everything else lays on and that cupcake base (the cake) is the bulk of the community and in our case, that foundation is our relationship with Christ. It comes first before everything else and dare I say it, if it is not right, then chances are that nothing else is going to be right either. It will all feel a little off, you can't quite put your finger on it, but it just doesn't come together as well as it does when our first and priority relationship is taken care of. This is where you must ask yourself, "Am I deeply rooted in my relationship with the Lord? Am I spending time with Him, in His Word, listening to His voice, and talking with Him each day?"

This layer is so important. Most of you already know that, but I also know that many in ministry still struggle with their quiet time. Oh, it's not something that is really talked about in public, but privately they struggle. After decades in the ministry, I have seen this firsthand and am hesitant to admit it, but for the sake of transparency you need to know that this is something that I struggled with as a pastor, a pastor's wife, a ministry leader, and whatever other hat I was wearing at the time.

You see, we can get so busy being "in" the ministry and doing the work "for" God that we forget that before anything else He simply desires a relationship "with" us. This is not about us doing things for Him but simply resting in and being with Him. The amazing thing is that our Heavenly Father modeled community with and for us. After all, He is Father, Son, and Holy Spirit—three-in-one and they are in constant and perfect community with each other.

Before we move on to the other layers of the community cupcake analogy, let's talk for a minute and get real practical about finding some solutions for any personal lack of community with Christ. What does your quiet time look like? Are you spending time in His Word just to get to know Him better? Do you spend time listening to His voice?

I know, I know—these are the same things we often tell others, but let's turn the light on ourselves for a minute. For us to lead those He brings into our path with excellence and with Christ-like character, we need to make sure we are grounded in the Word personally. You know that old saying when you are on a flight and they do the safety speech, "You need to put on your oxygen mask before helping others." This is the same thing.

One of the things that this season of the pandemic has allowed me to do is to spend so much more time in my daily quiet time. I'd strongly encourage you to shore up this connection before you move on to connection with others because the reality is that we can't lead others where we're we've not been or aren't going.

I love the verse in Joshua 1:8 (NLT) where it says, "Study this Book of Instruction continually. Meditate on it day and night so you will be sure to obey everything written in it. Only then will you prosper and succeed in all you do." This was the Lord's charge to Joshua after Moses died and it's a great reminder for us as we lead in the Church.

We cannot lead (at least not for long) without a fresh daily infusion from our Father. Yes, we can "get by" on our own for a bit, maybe even a season, but then we end up relying on ourselves and our own abilities which are never enough to do everything God has planned. I am not sure about you, but I no longer want to lead on my own; I want to be a leader that leads in tandem with Christ. I need Him to direct my steps and lead the way. As much as I like to lead, in this case, it is better to let Him lead while we just follow.

Community with Family

Okay, now that we have a good solid firm foundation for our beautiful cupcake, we are going to add in the next layer which is the icing. If you are still licking your fingers from the cupcake description earlier, then chances are you are still thinking about some buttercream icing . . . no judgment here, I am too. For our discussion the icing is just that—the layer that goes on top of the foundation. So, if our foundation is Christ, the icing is our family. They are the next most important community in our well-rounded life. You can have a giant layer of icing if you come from a big family, or a thin layer, but either way, after your community with God these are the people, you are going to want to pour into and develop.

As women who live, love, and lead in whatever area of ministry God has us in right now, this is one area that can sometimes get a little off balance if we are not intentional and careful. Apart from loving God with all your heart and soul and mind (Matthew 22:37), which is our first commandment, the second is to "love your neighbor as yourself" (Matthew 22:39 NLT). In this case our neighbor is not just the person across the street, it is also the people in our house and in our family.

Here's the thing, and I am going to tread lightly here, we can get so busy doing the ministry that we can forget that there is ministry that needs to happen inside our homes. As a matter of fact, I would argue that our family is our very first ministry. If you are married, then you were chosen to be your husband's wife. If you have kids, then you were chosen to be your children's mother. No one else has that title for those people, and it is a high calling. Depending on your ministry and the pace at which things happen in your organization, life can get hectic, frenzied, and chaotic quickly. And if this is what it looks like in your professional life then, as I said before and because I've been there - Don't sacrifice your family on the altar of ministry. They are not secondary to the work you are doing for the Church.

This is why it is so important that we are deeply rooted in Christ first. Otherwise, it is far too easy to be swept away by the current of this world and think that your family will understand and that the work you are doing is more important than being a wife and mom. Yes, there will be times and seasons while you lead that the ministry might be all consuming and require extra time and attention. But those seasons should have a distinct start and end, and it should not always be the case that your family must continue to take the back seat. Your work at the church is important, but your role as wife and mom is also important. I never want to minimize either because I've done both. I stayed home and raised our kids for nine years, then felt the call to full time ministry and went to work while they were in school. It is a juggle, and it is never perfect. Please hear me on that, it is never always balanced, but there are rhythms to it and once you settle in and find your rhythm, which usually depends on school years, ages, and stages of your kids' lives, you can start to predict those seasons a bit and come up with a plan.

If you are at all like me, you are a get it done overachiever. It's not a bad thing obviously because we are the people moving the implementation of ministry programs and processes forward but seeking to satisfy that drive can send your family straight to the back seat. This is probably my one biggest regret after decades in the ministry. I was so driven, so motivated, and so inspired by what I was doing and what the church was doing, that I unintentionally made the church my icing instead of my family and honestly, at that point, my foundation was a bit rocky as well. So much time doing the work of the ministry and not actually just sitting in His presence left me, as well as my family, worn out, hurt, and in desperate need of rest from the church.

Kids grow quickly, and time marches on even if you don't take some much-needed time to spend with your family. Don't miss out! Get creative! Part of the beauty of ministry life is that in a lot of ways there is flexibility. As we talked about in the moms in ministry chapter, figure out what your non-negotiables are for your family and then talk with your leadership team to see how you can make it a win-win for everyone. But above all, please prioritize the importance of regular and meaningful connection with your family while in ministry.

As I said, it's a balancing act to get everything where it belongs, but the bottom line is God first and then your family, not your job, not your ministry title, not anything else.

Okay, so we have our cake (our foundational community with God), and a nice thick layer of icing (our community with our family), and now we add in the sprinkles (our community with friends). Ah yes, this order is important because too many sprinkles effect the flow (or taste), and without a firm foundation our lives and ministry become all about us.

Community with Friends

Right about now you are probably thinking to yourself, "Friends? Who has time for friends? There are things to do, and I am barely keeping up as it is." Or you might even be thinking, "Is it even possible to have real friends when you are in the ministry?" My answer to both is yes and yes. Yes, there is time for friendship and yes you can have real friends while you are leading, serving, and doing all the things that you do each day.

It's so easy for your connection with friends to fall by the wayside of the demands of ministry and family. I get it, you are busy, they are busy, and life is a little chaotic right now. But guess what? It's always going to be a bit chaotic because you're in ministry. Don't miss the opportunity to take this amazing journey with other women. Sure, it requires some coordination and some flexibility, but it is so worth it—for you as well as for them.

Here's why it's so important, we need other people in our lives. Yes, we need that firm foundation in our relationship with Christ, and yes, we need a good, strong healthy family, but we also need other people that are going to go on this journey of life alongside us. You need people who can come with you and lighten the load, either by helping you carry it or by alleviating some of the stress and pressure building up in your world.

Friend is a funny word. Some of us think of it and it brings a great big smile to our face. Others of us will hear the word and it might make us cringe a bit. Let's face it. People are messy, but so are you.

We know from Scripture that no one is perfect, not even one (Romans 3:10), so we don't have to pretend to be perfect and have it all together, and we will not find a perfect friend. And you know the old saying, "If they are perfect, chances are they won't pick you to be their friend." Ouch, okay, that one hurt a bit, I know, but I'm trying to make the point that yes, it can get messy because no one is perfect, and yet if you've had a good friend, you know it can also be incredible as well.

I think this is why I believe it's crucial to have these three relationships of community in the proper order, first our relationship with God, next our relationship with our family, and then (after the other two are good and settled) we can bring friends into our lives. The reality is that at this point we are probably going to be better friends as well.

*"Alone we can do so little;
together we can do so much."* — Helen Keller[11]

Ok, so you get that we need these "sprinkles" in our lives, but how are you to find them and what should you be looking for in a friend? I think it will be different for each of us depending on the age and stage we are at in our lives as well as that of our family unit at that time. Here's what I know, though, the Bible lists "friends" over 200 times which leads me to believe that this is a very big deal. And if you want to get technical for a minute, let's look at the Trinity (Father, Son, and Holy Spirit). They are in community and constant connection with each other, so if it's that important to our Creator, then it's worth us taking some time to uncover these connections in our own personal lives.

Let's look at Jesus himself. He had twelve people, most likely they were friends, that He spent His life with, three of which were labeled as closest to Him and one that was like a brother. So, if Jesus, God in the flesh, had people (friends) around Him, don't you think we can learn from His example and build friends around us in our life?

In my experience I believe there are a couple types of friends that we should have in our lives: those who know us, and those who know us deeply (like Jesus' three). These deeper friendships are not numbered in the hundreds, they are a smaller group that gets you, has your back, will pray for you, and call you out when needed—not because they want to but because they love you enough to speak the truth to you. These friends can be in your church or organization, and that is important because they see and know your everyday reality. But I would also encourage you to find friendships that are outside of your local church community. They can be found at Bible studies or online groups, but whoever they are, they are not "in" your church business. They simply share your faith and like, respect, and admire you for you, not for what you do at the church or because you might be married to one of the pastors at their church.

In my own life I have had a group of women that I've been with in small groups in some way, shape, or form for almost fifteen years. Over that time we've ebbed and flowed in the seasons of life, walked through some fire storms that left us burned and battle weary (ministry can do that to you at times), and yet, through it all, they loved us, prayed for us, encouraged us, and held us up when we needed it. This group can pretty much say anything to me because I know that they love me and only want what's best for me, which gives them the right (in my mind) to be able to call me out when needed, and I love and respect them even more for it.

I love this quote (and I am sure you've heard it before) from Jim Rohn that says, "You are the average of the five people you spend the most time with."[12] So choose wisely!

In a bit I will talk more about how important it is to have friendships and connections outside of your church family, but for now it matters more to me that you see how vital these relationships and friends are for your life and ministry. We are not called to go at this life alone, but with God, our family, and our friends on our side (Ecclesiastes 4:9-12). We are more prepared to go, do, and be all that God created us to be when we have the right people beside us.

Who do you have in your life that can speak the truth to you? To whom do you speak the truth? Don't neglect the importance of these vital connections; like I said, they are the sprinkle on our cupcakes. They color our world, make it a little brighter, and bring some joy and excitement.

"I've learned that people will forget what you said, people will forget what you did, but people will never forget how you made them feel." — Maya Angelou[13]

So, what do you do if you don't have these friends in your life right now? You start praying for them immediately. You start preparing your heart for these divine connections.

If you do already have friends like this in your life, let them know how much they mean to you. Don't delay, don't wait another minute, send them a text and tell them how grateful you are that they are in your life. I'll wait. Yes, go ahead and text them now. It might seem silly but let this serve as your reminder that these friendships are important and need to be nurtured just like your relationship with Christ and your family. I'm not suggesting your friendships are more important. Misappropriating their importance would just give you an upside-down cupcake, which nobody likes because you got everything out of order. And your life and ministry could not support being upside down for long, could it? That's why it's in the order that it is. I'm just saying your friendships are worth your gratitude and investment.

This brings me to a brief word of caution, however, when creating connections—whether with your family or friends—please remember that relationships should be reciprocated. Give as much as you receive, if not more. I am sure this sounds confusing, but I would advocate for both being cautious yet also being generous. Pray and seek clarity if you are wrestling with this specific part of your connections with friends. If done well, your connections pray for you, encourage you, challenge you, inspire you, listen to you, and allow you to be the best version of yourself.

Community takes time, intentionality, and planning, but when you do all those things it is so worth it.

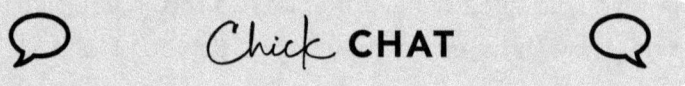

Real, practical advice on being a female leader in the ministry and making sure you have time for friends.

I schedule time on my calendar each week to meet with one special friend. We have time set aside and make it a priority. With other friends, it is a monthly date. When it is on the calendar it demonstrates the importance of our time together. – Sabrina

I have a small group of friends that decided on scheduling dinner and birthday cake, so we calendar it. – Amy

Schedule a face-to-face lunch twice a month and a Friday phone call just to check in twice a month.
— DeDe

Let your friends serve with you! Friends have worked my book table, recorded my presentation for me, and helped me haul stuff. Plus, then we sit together traveling to the event, usually at the event, and the whole ride home. -Gena

Intentional friendships take intentional effort. Be the friend to others that you crave. – Noreen

Don't ditch friends for the sake of ministry. Bring 'em with you or schedule time together and don't miss it.
– Dianne

Pursue the friends who are pursuing hard after Christ too—they will bless you and be with you in the little and the big things. It's not the crowds you want but the safe circle. Pursue friends who see the woman behind the ministry leader. Keep in touch during the week thru a scheduled phone call day, or prayer requests thread throughout the week. – Rehana

Lead relationally. Then your team are your friends. As for best friends, I say don't limit yourself to a geographical setting. Sometimes our best friends are rocking their corner of the world in another state or country. Schedule time with friends, like you would schedule a date with your spouse or schedule your devos. – Stephanie

Make time for good friends—it starts with an intention to invest time in someone else. It can be a text to encourage, a coffee chat to refresh, or a phone chat to catch up. You have to make time for it, but when you do it's all good and refreshing for the soul. – Roslyn

I put extra effort into my friendships outside of my church. The time with those folks never has to be wrapped up in the highs and lows of leading, church info, if they'll say yes to serving, etc. I just get to be me, and they know me beyond this job or work season. – Pamm

Staying connected to friends in ministry is critical because we all need encouragement. I schedule time with friends on purpose. I make the time. If I don't make the time, I will not do it because something else will always come up. I have a few friends with whom I schedule this time together. We build each other up and pray for one another as well. These friends keep me on track. They share life but also ministry, and I learn from them, as well as they from me. Ministry chicks need to stick together! – Dawn

Champion Female Leaders Around You

Buckle up, friends, because here's where the rubber starts to meet the road. No really, we need to take a few minutes and talk, like 100% straight talk about being a champion for other female leaders in your organization and around you. We do not need to spend one more moment tearing anyone down (I'm not talking about you, of course; none of us would do that, but we've seen it happen around us).

We also need to stop comparing ourselves, our ministry, our social media presence, or our . . . whatever you want to fill in this blank, to anyone else's.

You are you.

They are not you.

They are themselves.

You are not called to their race.

They are not called to yours.

Even if it might "look" the same, it is not the same, because your experiences, insight, age, stage of life and everything in between make it 100% unique to you. And the same is true for them.

So, let's stop comparing ourselves to someone else.

Can I also just take a moment to talk about the "queen bee" thing that I've seen (and heard of) happening in some of our organizations? You know the queen bee. She is reigning "queen" female leader of the organization, and she will not tolerate any others trying to take her spot. She looks down on and holds back other female leaders around her, most usually because of her own insecurity. I wish I was making her up, but I've seen her, I've worked with her, and let me tell you that as a strong female leader it was not fun to be around her.

The funny thing is that most of the time the attitude of queen bees comes from a scarcity mentality. This is the idea that there is one and only one spot available for a female leader and she's got it. Because of this, her time and energy are spent keeping others down and holding them back. She plays small and does not allow any other women in the organization a chance to lead well.

Let's flip the script on that. Instead of having a scarcity mentality as female leaders, why don't we look at ministry—or whatever we are called to do in Jesus' name—with an abundance filter even if the reality is that there is not a lot of room for female leaders in senior leadership. We, yes, *we* can change how we lead. We can become champions for female leaders around us. We can move over and make room at the table for other women who are growing into their leadership influence.

Let's park here for a minute. We have a chance to open doors for female leaders around us. Whether the doors are opened to them by anyone else, *we* can open the doors to which we have access. We can let younger leaders into our sphere of influence. We can bring emerging female leaders to our meetings. We can invite other females to join us as we work through decisions, meet with other leaders or prepare budgets. These are all opportunities to teach, train, mentor, guide, or whatever you want to call it; I simply call it opening the door.

For so long, so many of us have been held back locked behind the other side of the door. We may have fought to get to where we are, we may have just done our time, we may have had to work harder, smarter, longer than others to get to where we are, but we can also decide that the women behind us don't have to go through all the junk we had to go through to get to that point. I know you might be saying, "But some of that hard work and striving gave us grit." That is true for sure. There's a tenacity element that just happens from having to go through the stuff to get to the other side. But do we really want others to wait twenty years to get into positions of influence and purpose? Because that is pretty close to the amount of time it took for me to get to this point. I don't want that for the emerging leaders behind me.

I know that it can be hard, even for us as women, to break through generations of stereotypes. Depending on the culture of your organization and the overall understanding and acceptance of diversity, equity, and inclusion, this might just now be a topic that is being addressed. Be patient and don't give up hope. You might just be the person that God placed in that organization, dare I say it, for such a time as this. We can't expect change to happen without actively being a part of it.

Being an agent of change will be difficult at times because it is not easy being a trailblazer, but if God has you in that role, there is a specific reason for it and He will prepare and equip you for exactly what you need at each stage of the journey. Change takes time and it's important to prayerfully consider if you are ready to be the trailblazer for the long haul. And you must decipher your particular part in making this change. Are you the one planting the seed or watering it (1 Corinthians 3:6)? Someone else might have started that momentum and God has you there to water it and continue to support it.

As I mentioned just a bit ago, we are even battling stereotypes within our own gender. It can be hard for some women to see other women as leaders. For some reason or another it grates on their nerves and makes them uncomfortable. They might not even realize they have this bias; they just know that something bugs them about you. Yep, I have experienced this as well. Coming in as a leading female on a male dominated staff immediately put a target on my back with some of the other women on staff. They were used to holding only the administrative roles and responsibilities that women, in the past, held in that organization so they really wrestled with the idea of me as a ministry leader. I tried not to take it personally, although if I am honest, it sure felt personal. The hard part was that while I would champion and encourage them in what God had called and created them to do, it was not reciprocated simply because there was a gender bias at work. And in their defense, they may not have even realized they had a bias about other women until I came in and rocked the boat a bit with my new role.

Please hear me on this, I love the administrative teams that I have worked with. I loved them as people, and heaven knows we need those people to do what they do (and love to do) to help make churches and organizations run. God did not wire me that way, so I celebrate that they are using the gifts God gave them with their whole heart. I cannot be inauthentic to myself and try to be more like them just to make them like me or to fit it. I honestly feel like that is a disservice to who God created you and I to be. I think it was Dr. Suess who said, "Why try to fit in when you were born to stand out."[14]

So dear friend, stop trying to fit everyone else's role for you and start trying to be the best you that God created you to be. If you are in an environment where it feels heavy, hard, and a little tough right now, the best thing you can do is to prepare yourself, cover yourself in prayer, and make sure you have a safe place (this is yet another reason why it is so important to have those layers of the cupcake) to vent, cry if you need to, bounce ideas off of, and gather the strength you need to keep on keeping on.

The only word of caution I would say to you is this, if the environment is unhealthy, and I mean unhealthy for you as an individual, then prayerfully consider if God has you there for a reason or if He is trying to show you that it is okay to move on now. I am not saying you just up and quit if or when things get hard, but an unhealthy organization that eats away at your identity in Christ in some way, shape, or form, and is just not good for you, may be an indicator that it's just not a good fit. I am not saying that the organization is necessarily bad, it may just not be a fit for you. And that is okay. There have been seasons in which I have walked away from organizations because they were not a good fit for me or I for them. You don't have to always push a rock uphill to make it move.

Perhaps, and hopefully, it's not like this for you in your specific organization. If that's the case, stop and celebrate that. Make sure your team, leadership, and others know just how grateful you are for their willingness to listen, learn, and allow women to lead the way God created them to lead. And then please don't take it for granted. You have an opportunity right there in front of you to exponentially grow, develop, and lead more female leaders in an environment where it is conducive to their growth in a healthy way. What a gift that is!

In your organization, think through how you can be a champion for other female leaders.

Here are some examples:

» Invite them to your meetings.

» Meet with them once a week.

» Give them space to come and ask questions.

» Listen to them. What are they learning and what are they struggling with on their leadership journey?

» Share books, podcasts, and online resources that have been helpful for you as a female leader.

Another way you can be *for* other female leaders is to network with other female leaders outside of your organization. I'll take it a step further and strongly encourage you to not only network with these leaders, but to invest in inviting a few of them to your friendship circle. No, you aren't going to exchange friendship bracelets, but I mean, hey, if you want to you can. This network of female leaders outside of your church can be crucial to your development as well as your own mental health and well-being. Here's why. I have that amazing group of friends that I mentioned earlier. I love them dearly and they love me, but they do not, and I mean do not, get what I do and why I do it. They are businesswomen, teachers, flight nurses, and even stay at home wives, but they do not understand the stress and pressure that is unique to my calling as a woman in ministry.

They try and I love them for it, but they can go to church and not have to worry about what they say, how they say it, or how it is heard or perceived. They simply go, attend, love it, and leave. For those of us in the ministry it is not that easy, and it never has been. I'm hoping one day it will be, which is why I am such a big advocate for having these friendships (not just networking connections) with women who do what you do outside of your church family.

One of my biggest mistakes early on in my ministry career was that all my friends were only at my church. If they, or even I, moved on, then the friendship just sort of disappeared. It wasn't because of any ill will or anything, but because I was so focused on my local church. That is something I fixed about five years ago. I knew that I was missing out by only having friends in my circle. Yes, it's important to have friends *in* your church family because they understand the world that you work and life in, but as women in ministry, I would highly encourage you to connect and build friendships with women outside of your local church family.

From a networking perspective it's also great. We share ideas, tips, trade equipment, studies, etc. It's also wonderful to have someone to bounce ideas around with and share victories as well as the hard stuff that happens each day in the ministry. I've had some of my best ideas and biggest breakthroughs happen at lunch with a friend who does what I do at another church. It's been hugely beneficial for me, and hopefully for them. I can cheer her on, encourage her, and support her in prayer in a way that she knows that I "get" it and she can do the same for me. This kind of network of leaders will encourage you when ministry gets tough. To be quite honest, these friendships have given me some of my best ideas in my ministry, and they have become some of my greatest friends. Again, I would never have just run into these women or the relationships we've formed on my own.

In fact, these connections never just happen. They take time, lots of prayer, and intentionality. You also have to make space in your calendar and life for these friendships, but again, it's so worth it. Over the two decades that I have been in the ministry this has been a constant for me. I am a big believer in the big "C" church as well as the little "c" local church. I love the local church, but I love the big "c" church even more. This is a kingdom mindset that takes the lid off comparison and competition. The church down the street is *not* your competition. It's life, the world—the beach, the mountains, sports, lifestyle choices etc., that are your competition. It's composed of all the things getting people's attention and keeping it. Those are the things that are your competition, not other churches in your community. So why not link arms and share ideas to support and encourage each other since you're all on the same mission?

Real Ministry Chick Experience

from Carrie Ann Williams

Years ago, I attended a workshop on leadership. It was led by a prominent male leader well known among church circles. I remember walking in so excited about all that I would learn and apply to my leadership and life. I expected best practices and his own personal "secret sauce" that made him the amazing leader he was. And I got exactly what I expected and a whole lot that I didn't. As I sat and listened to this man speak on leadership, I found that he addressed the room in "male gender" terms with lots of "he's and him's". This is the kind of thing that I usually didn't notice or get bothered by, but there I was, getting a bit disturbed by his lack of awareness or intentionality to address the 25% of attendees in the room who were female.

As the workshop continued, he offered solutions to relationships and networking, which again, were addressed to the men in the room. Solutions like "find your counterpart in other churches and take them to play golf", "invite your counterparts to lunch", "join a network or find a coach". All of this was great advice but the problem for me as a woman was I don't play golf, all my counterparts in my city were men —so striking a personal relationship with them over lunch would have its share of complications, the networks that I was aware of were all male-led with the majority (if not all) being male, and every coach I had looked into hiring were men.

So, you may be asking, "What's the big deal? Can you not learn from men or be in relationship with men other than your spouse?" My answer is I had plenty of those. I was oozing with male options to seek out for my leadership and ministry development. What I was lacking were women who sat in my same seat, women who had been there done that, women who were leading at the same level I was, and women who understood what it's like to be a woman in vocational ministry. I left that workshop frustrated and honestly a bit angry that it felt like the male leading the conversation left me and the other women out.

That workshop I attended began a journey of revealing a deep longing I had to be surrounded by women who I could relate to, learn from, and walk with while networking and collaborating. This led me to seek God like crazy about how to not only fill the gap for myself, but also for the many women I knew who were in the same situation. My prayers led to a very vivid dream, that I know without a doubt, was from the Lord. In my dream I was sitting with two of my closest friends and telling them, "I have to start this thing called The Truth Republic."

I remember clearly the passion that I was feeling and the strong knowledge that if I didn't start it, I would be in direct disobedience to the Lord.

I woke up from the dream and wrote in my journal the words "TRUTH REPUBLIC, what is it?". Over the coming months God would unravel a beautiful picture of a movement that would help fill the gap for women when it comes to fulfilling His calling on their lives. Fast forward four years, and The Truth Republic is a living, thriving movement that has only just begun to touch the surface of filling this gap I described.

The Truth Republic is making Jesus known by equipping and empowering women to fulfill their calling. We are an aggregator of resources, knowledge, and relationships—from women to women—for the sake of the Gospel. We are bridging the gap that exists by platforming the voices and learnings from experienced women and making those voices available to be heard and learned from. We tend to focus on relationships in all that we do, opening pathways for women to connect, learn from one another, and advance the kingdom together. Ladies, we need each other! We need to be present for one another, supportive, encouraging, making the way easier and better for each other as we forge ahead in our calling.

One of my favorite things we do as part of The Truth Republic is the quarterly Leaders Round Table Community. It is a group of amazing female leaders from around the country, like Melissa, that God connected me with in some form or fashion. Women that I have plenty to learn from, women who are spending their lives making Jesus known, women I call friends. As God introduced each one of these women into my life, I found myself longing to connect them to one another and that is where the community began. Over 40 female leaders are invited into this intimate and life-giving intentional community. Every quarter those of us who can jump online to see each other's faces, connect, listen, pray, encourage, and I walk away so fueled every time.

Ladies, I want to challenge you to find your people and join them. Your girl tribe, your lady league, your sisterhood, whatever you want to call them . . . find them. Pray them into your life and pursue them. Community is a must, it is part of our wiring as we were created in the image of God, who on week one of creation determined He would create a man and a woman to commune with in a garden. Stepping into this gap will not only fill a need you have personally but it will do the same for the many women who need deep rooted, God breathed, life-giving, calling equipping, empowering relationships.

QUICK *Tips*

Here are some practical solutions to grow and develop your connection and community with Christ:

» YouVersion Bible App (by yourself or with your significant other, family members, or even friends). The beauty of this is that it is on your phone so that means it's pretty much always with you.

» Silence and solitude (see Ruth Haley Barton resources)

» Prayer Journal

» Start your day with a worship song that moves you.

» Start your day with God *first*. I do a quick glance at my phone first thing in the morning to make sure that my kids didn't text or need me, then I clear all the notifications. It makes my husband crazy that I do that, but I do not want to be distracted by all those notifications at the top of my screen while I am in my quiet time.

» Bible study—Just attend, watch, or listen at your local church or even online. (Right Now Media[15] has some amazing free Bible studies online.)

So, let's get real practical for a moment to see how you can develop your connection with your family:

✓ Have a family day on the calendar each week.

✓ Plan at least one family meal a week where everyone eats together and puts their phones in the other room (yes—even you!).

✓ Talk with your family and see what some of the non-negotiables for them are. At each age and stage of their life this is going to look different, but oftentimes their needs and desires are different than what you might have anticipated. Don't try to figure this out on your own. Ask your family and see what they need from you in this season of their life.

✓ If you are married, make date day/night a priority with your spouse. Long after the kids are grown and leave the nest it will be you and your spouse. Build and foster that relationship now so that you have a marriage that will last through the seasons and transitions of life. It is also incredibly important as a married woman in ministry to have a good strong healthy marriage. You are leading and will become a target for the enemy in several different ways, and your marriage will be one of those targets. Work on solidifying it every day to build stamina and awareness, so that you will be able to withstand the enemy's attacks.

✓ Go through the practical solutions in the section titled "the people you are raising".

✓ Whenever you are with your family, focus on being fully present as much as you can.

Practical solutions for developing your community of friends:

✓ Write down your 5 closest friends' names.

✓ If you don't have close friends, pray and ask God to bring them into your life.

✓ Plan some time to connect with your friends. Go ahead and check your calendar and throw out options to meet—don't just say "we need to get together." Provide one another with options of when you can get together.

✓ Pray for your friends often. They are praying for you, so pick a day a week and always pray for that one friend and rotate each day with the name of a friend for whom you are praying.

✓ Put yourself out there to connect with others and work on being a good friend to them while you wait for God to send you the kind of friends you are praying for.

What are some practical ways you can start to make these connections outside of your church family? Here are some ideas:

✓ Look up five churches near you and find out who does what you do at their church, then reach out via email or a phone call and see if they might want to connect. Buy them coffee, lunch, or whatever. Just be generous. Let them know what you are doing and offer yourself as a resource. Everyone is looking for new ideas. It's a brave new world right now and we are all learning a little on the fly. Why not share what you've been learning.

✓ Send a card to the "staff" team at five other churches in your area or within 150 miles of you and simply tell them that you prayed for them (which, please if you say you prayed, please take the time to pray) and you are grateful for the impact they are making in the community.

    ✓ We need to be cheerleaders *for* each other, not just our own team. You'd be surprised how other church teams respond when you do this. And yes . . . I've done this before, many times.

Chapter 7

YOU WERE MADE FOR MORE: OWN YOUR LEADERSHIP

You were made for more and in the last section we really dug into the idea of finding your community. We are going to switch gears a bit and talk specifically about you! It's time for you to own your leadership and your gifts. During the Global Leadership Network Summit in 2018, Pastor Craig Groeschel said, "Everybody has influence."[16] I love that quote and I believe that not only is it true, but maybe even more so in today's world. Just look at YouTube, Instagram, TikTok and all the other social networks used to have influence.

People who normally would not have had that kind of influence now have millions of followers and people connecting with them through their content. They are leading whether they even realize it or not. But chances are that you and I are not going to have 1 million+ followers in anything, and hey, if you do, please give a shout out about your girl and this book you're reading. Anyway, here's the deal. You are a leader.

You have people that are watching, listening, learning, and probably even following you. I highly doubt you would have picked up this book if you didn't. It may not be the platform or size of platform that you dreamed of or thought you would have at this point in your life, but you do have influence and it is way past time for you to *own* your leadership.

What do I mean when I say, "own your leadership"? Well, for far too long, many female leaders have hidden their gifts and skills in silent fear that they may be "seen" or "heard" or come across as "too much". I have always been "too much." As a matter of fact, my youngest son just said to me the other day, "Mom, you're so extra" and he didn't mean it as a compliment . . . but I chose to see it that way anyway. Remember that young 4th grade girl in the beginning of the book? The one to whom her 4th grade teacher asked, "Who do you think you are?" Yeah, that girl. That's me and that statement has haunted me most of my adult life. One simple statement to a young impressionable "too much" girl unintentionally put a governor on my "too muchness." A governor, if you don't know, is that thing on your car that keeps you from going too fast. (I live in a house of boys, so I can attest that this is a real thing.) That statement set me back for decades. It has taken years of counseling, coaching, maturing, and personal growth to allow me to shed that governor from my "too muchness", and it is now being replaced by this "go for it and take on the world" spirit that has always been there but was buried too deep to even remember who I was so long ago.

> *"Mountaintops inspire leaders,*
> *but valleys mature them."* — Winston Churchill[17]

This, my friend, is what I mean by owning your leadership. If you have always been a leader, and yet you find yourself holding back in meetings, gatherings, and other places where you can make a difference, then it is time for you to own your leadership as well. Does that mean you have freedom to unleash your "too muchness" all over everyone? No, that wouldn't be kind. There's a level of maturity, growth, and depth that, when partnered with us owning our leadership, is truly remarkable.

There are many of you reading this right this moment who have more inside of you. More ideas, more creative input, more abilities, more you name it. Whatever it is, it's completely unique to you, and yet you are holding back. You don't want to be seen as "too much", or worse, as a female leader, you don't want to be seen as aggressive, unyielding, or dare I say it . . . the B word. For some reason it is 100 percent ok for a man to be strong, confident, aggressive, and even unyielding, and people will applaud him for being a great leader, but if a woman exhibits those same qualities, she is often labeled as uncompromising and difficult.

The hard part about that is that she is judged not only by her male counterparts at work, but also from the female counterparts at work as we talked about in the last chapter. It is hard to lead with strength and confidence, and at the same time, be completely misunderstood. Therefore, it is so important to have that firm foundation in Christ, a healthy family relationship, and those all-important sprinkles of friendships in your life.

One of the things that has been helpful for me over the years as I have started to own my leadership is this balance of holy confidence and healthy humility. It is a fine line because so many of us can veer over to humility but it's not really a healthy humility, we shrug it off, point the victory to someone else, and deflect or negate the work we've done, which is not really humility. Instead, it's almost a false humility when we minimize the gifts and skills God has placed in us. That is not really honoring God, is it? And as for holy confidence, we know things can quickly get off balance when it is all about us, what we bring to the table, and what we can do on our own. We want to be confident, for sure, but holy confidence is righteous because it makes it all about Him.

The holy confidence is Christ in me, the gifts He has given me, and the insights He shares with me. Have you ever watched baseball players? Before the pitch is made, they get in a ready stance, knees bent, eyes forward, and glove at the ready. This is how I describe holy confidence. You know who you are, what your role is, and what you bring to the table, and your eyes are forward, ready for whatever God sends you to do. That is what holy confidence looks like. It's you walking into a meeting, not having to prove yourself, not trying too hard, not trying to have all the answers, but simply in the ready position, confident of the gifts and skills God has given you, and able to respond when you are prompted by Him or by your leaders.

It's the coolest thing to see a woman who has a holy confidence and healthy humility. She knows who she is, and she knows *Whose* she is, and she is not afraid to be all her and give Him all the glory. How amazing would it be to be a woman with a holy confidence and healthy humility who champions other women along the way.

This is why it is so critical for you as a leader to first lead yourself well. Yes, I know, you have probably heard that phrase before, but do you really get what it means? Do you put it to practice? Are you really leading yourself well or are you going with the flow and wherever the wind blows you? And that's not a shot at you, it's the result of honest reflection.

The hard part is that if we are not intentionally driving ourselves somewhere, we will drift to places we don't even want to go and end up far away from our goals, dreams, or even tasks. This is 100 percent natural, and it happens to the best of us. I have often jokingly said that I woke up and I was ten years older. And while that didn't really happen, I was awake but stuck for far too long in the cycle of just making it through each day.

Life was coming at me from all angles, and it was all that I could do just to keep all the plates spinning. There was work, husband, kids, kids' activities and homework, ministry, my role at the church, friendships, family stuff, doctor appointments . . . life. And in different seasons, you might just survive and make it through the day. But as a leader who is learning to own her leadership, you need to wake up and stop letting life and ministry and stuff just happen to you. You can either be run over or you can drive. I would much prefer to drive than be run over. How about you?

So, what does leading yourself well look like? Here's the hard part. I don't think there is one definitive answer to this question because there are so many factors at play and it really does depend on all those things. However, there are a few things that can be universal to each of us no matter what age or stage of life we are in to lead ourselves well. Are we spending time in the Word? Are we taking care of ourselves? Are we going to our annual doctor's appointments, taking vitamins, drinking water, and moving our body? Often, these are the very things we tend to put off doing because there are so many other more pressing things going on in our lives. Do not do this. There is only one of you. Some of the roles you fill (wife and mom) can only be filled by you. Part of leading yourself well is taking care of yourself. I'm not saying you have to run a marathon or bench free weights at the gym, but hey, if you want to do that and it connects you to God and you enjoy nature and find it takes care of your body, then go for it. I will be cheering you on from the sidelines. Just kidding, I will be cheering you on from the internet, but you know what I mean.

Leading yourself well also means getting a real picture of who you are, not just who you think you are or who others say you are, but who God says you are. Yes, I know,

I'm back at being in the Word, but friends, leading in the church or being in ministry can mess with your spiritual life if you are not grounded. And yes, I am aware that was a big bold statement I just made, but I have seen it in my career, and unfortunately, I have lived it as well. You must know *whose* you are first. Then you can figure out *who* you are after that.

Once you spend time in the Word, taking care of yourself, going to all your appointments (yes . . . even the ones that are not fun), then you can start to tackle leading yourself well in other ways. What are you reading? What are you listening to? Who are you allowing to speak into your life, leadership, and ministry?

One of the biggest breakthroughs I had in my ministry career was when I did a two-day life planning retreat with Kadi Cole. She took me through the process, and while it was painful and emotional at times, when we finished at the end of day two, I had a great big aha! moment and was able to walk away with a clear understanding of why I exist. I know you are wondering what it is, so here goes. "I exist to encourage unseen people, talents, and possibilities through connection, fun, and influencing actions to help others rise up and kick butt!!!" Yep, it says kick butt. And yes, it has three exclamation points, mostly because after two days of digging and heart work I felt it deserved and needed more than one exclamation point.

I know that not everyone reading this book is going to be able to do a two-day life planning retreat, so I'd love to share with you a few other things that I think will be helpful as you lead yourself better. The first thing I would suggest, and I realize that even in today's world that this might still be taboo, but it's been so vital to me is to get counseling.

Find yourself a good solid Christian counselor. A lot of churches have this benefit (counseling) in their handbook, and it is often a part of your benefits package. Do a little digging or consult with HR and see what is available to you because it is worth it. For almost the entire time that I have been in the ministry I have been in counseling and here's why. What we do as leaders in the Church is heavy stuff. It can be fun, exciting, and joyous, of course, but a lot of times we are walking with hurt people through the hard times in their life and this can be overwhelming at times. The stress of carrying other people's burdens can build up. This is where a good Christian counselor comes in. They can help you process what's going on in and around you in the ministry as well as help you process your own life stuff that may be happening at the same time. Matt and I have a monthly call with our counselors. It's a pulse check for how we are doing, how we are processing things, how we see Jesus, and so much more. For the first fifteen years in ministry, I went to counseling alone, but in these last few years, Matt joined me to talk through challenges in the ministry, life, marriage, parenting adult children, and lots of other thing with our counselors. Again, this is totally up to you, but it can be an excellent addition to leading yourself well.

*"One's philosophy is not best expressed in words;
it is expressed in the choices one makes . . .
and the choices we make are ultimately
our responsibility."* -Eleanor Roosevelt[18]

Another thing I would suggest to lead yourself well would be to identify any obstacles in your leadership. This requires that you take it a step further and determine if they are internal obstacles (self-sabotage, feelings of guilt, less than, etc.) or external obstacles (real barriers in your organization) that need to be addressed. You cannot move forward in health, healing, and growth if you are not fully aware of what's stopping you or holding you back. This is something that you could work on or through with a Christian coach. I am a big advocate for coaching and the benefits that working with a coach has on your leadership. Throughout my career I have been extremely blessed to have worked with some industry leaders in the ministry and they have helped me to move forward faster than I could have on my own. In fact, I've had many women in ministry seek my help in this area, so I started my own coaching and consulting company to be able to help other women experience breakthrough themselves.

Left on my own, I struggle with analysis paralysis. Questions like "What if I get it wrong?" and "What if I am not ready?" were regular contenders for my sanity. I was also my own obstacle at times when I hadn't put myself out there or stood up for myself for promotions, equal pay, etc.

A few years ago, I was talking with someone who said something that struck me funny about not asking me to do something or provide input on a specific situation for which I actually had experience. When I asked why, their response was a real eye opener for me. They said to me, "I never knew you did that, because you've never talked about it with me." My "false humility" had put up barriers in places where there were already some there, but the unknown experiences were a box that I put myself in. That stunk! After processing it for some time, I had finally had it so I scheduled a meeting with my boss to express my frustrations. The conversation was all kinds of awkward and my position wasn't necessarily received well, but I walked away from that meeting so proud of myself for finally stepping up and saying something.

Recently while doing a podcast interview with Susan Vandenheuvel,[19] she asked me how I began to grow my confidence. I absolutely loved that question because there's something under that question that implies that there was action taken. And there was. I began to grow in my confidence when I stopped worrying about what others thought about me, my gifts, my leadership, my title, whatever "me" things I had and who they said I was. It was intentional. It was work. It took time. But now, on this side of that digging and discovery, I can walk the line of humility *and* holy confidence. Do I always get it right? Not a chance, but I am way more aware and settled in my spirit than ever before.

What about the times when we catch ourselves starting to shrink back? If we were discussing it together, I would ask what makes you feel you need to shrink back and why you do it. Making yourself less is maddening and it doesn't help you, the organization, or the situation. After all, they hired you for a reason.

What does shrinking back look like? It's functioning from a dialed down version of yourself, either out of fear, insecurity, demands, experience, or even social cues. At work, that could manifest itself by staying quiet when you have ideas or experience. It could also involve something as simple as offering to take the notes at the meeting because you are the only female in the room. It's really settling for an inauthentic version of who you really are. In a lot of ways, I've done this over the years as a pastor's wife. If you take any of those personality tests, a pastor's wife is generally (but not always) hard to nail down because she spends most of her time trying to be "everything to everyone" while also trying really hard to "not be too much". Ugh—it's exhausting, overwhelming, and really quite lonely.

Real Ministry Chick Experience

from Dr. Angie Ward

Living Fully as a Female Leader

I've always been good at being "one of the guys." From an early age, I loved sports and outdoor activities, which put me more in the company of boys more than girls on the playground and in my neighborhood. I was also strong, tough, and I liked cars and mechanical stuff—which were also "guy things."[20]

As a young adult, I worked for several years as a sportswriter, again placing myself in the minority in terms of representation by sex. And then when I heard and followed God's call into vocational ministry, I entered another male-dominated world. At every stop on that journey—from my years in youth ministry, to my seminary studies, to my work with denominational leaders, to my doctoral program, to my teaching at a variety of Christian institutions—I've been the minority, a woman in a man's world.

For many, many years, I felt tension between who I was, and who I felt I was "supposed" to be. I just never felt like I fit in. As a seminary student, I felt more kinship with the men training to be pastors than with the seminary wives' fellowship, yet as a female I was the outlier in my classes. I became a pastor's wife, but I disliked the women's retreats I was expected to attend. No matter whether I was in groups of men or groups of women, I always felt like the odd (wo)man out.

Over the years I tried two different approaches to resolve this discomfort:

First, I tried to be one of the guys. Thanks to my experience in male-dominated environments, this was fairly easy. I did my best to blend in, to not be female in any distracting way. But even though I found some measure of professional success with this approach, I eventually realized I was cutting off parts of myself—parts of the whole self that God had created. The reality was that I was not a guy, nor should I try to be.

Second, I tried to not be a leader. I tried to be more domestic, less strong, less independent— whatever seemed to be culturally "acceptable" for women within contemporary evangelicalism. But this only made me feel more constricted and even less of my whole self. (Please note that none of this behavior was mandated or encouraged by my husband. He has always been the biggest champion for me being me, and continually reminds me that my uniqueness is why he married me.)

After far too many years of trying to be someone I was not, I finally heard the Holy Spirit's whispers to be who I am—and that I who I am is complex, full, beautiful, and complete in God's eyes. So, who am I?

1) I am a leader. Leadership is a critical part of who I am, not just what I do. I am not just a woman who leads; I am a leader through and through. It is how I am wired. It is the lens through which I view the world. But not only am I a leader . . . .

2) I am a female leader. I lead differently because I am a woman. I am fully a leader, and I am fully female. I don't need to be one of the guys, and I don't need to turn off or mute my leadership. I can and should bring both of these fully to the table, no matter what environment I am in. My brothers and sisters need all of me, whether they realize it or appreciate it or not.

Being a female leader often makes me a unicorn in a room. I don't easily fit into boxes and categories. Many people don't know what to do with me. But I've learned that this is their issue, not mine. All I can do is to continue to live into who and what God has created, called, and gifted me to be: a female leader.[21]

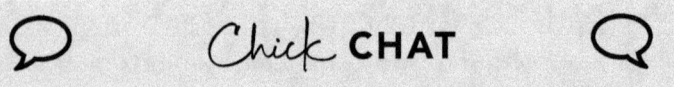

Chick CHAT

Real, practical advice on being a female leader in the ministry to develop your leadership so you can lead yourself and others better.

I think leadership development begins with mindset. Without a biblically-based mindset, we resort to our insecurities and bad habits. 1. Believe God created you to be a leader. If you don't believe it, you won't live it. 2. Realize to be a good leader, you need to be a good follower. You follow Jesus first. You also have to follow/work with other leaders in your ministry/workplace. 3) Be teachable. Always be willing to learn. 4) Be confident. God has put you in this place for a purpose. – Michelle

Make a commitment to develop your leadership. No one can be more committed to your development than you are. Your level of commitment is the most committed anyone will be (because you're the one doing the most work in the process.) Get a vision for your life, girlfriend. You got this! – Stephanie

Watch respected leaders around you. Watch what and how and why they do what they do. Ask them about why they do what they do. Adopt the best of what you see and leave the rest behind. Do not try to be them; instead adopt best practices that fit you, challenge you, and strengthen you as a leader.

– Dianne

Invest in yourself. Don't wait for someone to send you to a conference. Go yourself. Who cares if you are the only person there that is not a "staff member"? I've gone to conferences for pastors (and I have zero call to be a pastor) because of the leadership content there. Buy the book. Take the workshop. Mentor under other leaders. Don't wait for them to come to you. Seek them out. – Gena

I've been asking those I supervise, "Are you managing or are you leading?" There's a place for managing of course, but often we don't give ourselves permission to fully lead, innovate, or dream. – Amanda

QUICK *Tips*

Practical tips for owning your leadership:

✓ Spend some time prayerfully considering what may be some of your obstacles?

✓ Think of one thing you can do today to lead yourself well?

✓ Determine who from your team you could invest time in to help them in their leadership development.

✓ Prayerfully consider meeting with a Christian counselor to help uncover things that might hold you back as you lead yourself as well as others.

✓ You do have influence, so you need to determine what you still need to do to develop and nurture that influence.

✓ Find someone you respect and admire and ask if they would be available to meet with you for one hour once a month, or every other month for mentoring or even for professional coaching.

   ✓ If they agree, then respect their time by showing up (early) and prepared with questions. Buy their coffee or their lunch because they are giving up time to spend with you. The least you can do is to show your appreciation.

✓ If they do not have the time or are not available, then ask if you can send them an email with a list of questions and see if they have time for that. Anything would be helpful.

Chapter 8

YOU WERE MADE FOR MORE: TAKE YOUR STEP

If there is one sentence that I keep hearing from God over the last year it is, "Take your step." Think of it as my one word in a sentence form. Anyway, it has been a key driver for change for me and I think it can be for you as well. What is holding you back from taking your step? What fears, stressors, anxiety, or doubts keep you from living full out and chasing the dreams that He has given you? Oh, I know they are there, I've dealt with them for years in my own life. Which is why I know firsthand just how liberating this one sentence can be . . . Take your step, _____ (insert your name here).

Take your step of faith.

Take your step of obedience.

Take your step and put your feet in the water.

Take your step and watch what only God can do in your life and ministry.

In Joshua 3 there's an amazing story of taking the step that I would love to share with you.

Early in the morning Joshua and all the Israelites set out from Shittim and went to the Jordan,
where they camped before crossing over. After
three days the officers went throughout the camp,
giving orders to the people: 'When you see the
ark of the covenant of the Lord your God, and the
Levitical priests carrying it, you are to move out
from your positions and follow it. Then you will
know which way to go, since you have never been
this way before. But keep a distance of about two
thousand cubits[a] between you and the ark; do
not go near it.' Joshua told the people, 'Conse-
crate yourselves, for tomorrow the Lord will do
amazing things among you.' Joshua said to the
priests, 'Take up the ark of the covenant and pass
on ahead of the people.' So they took it up and
went ahead of them. And the Lord said to Joshua, 'Today I will begin to exalt you in the eyes of
all Israel, so they may know that I am with you as I
was with Moses. Tell the priests who carry the ark
of the covenant: 'When you reach the edge of the
Jordan's waters, go and stand in the river.' Joshua
said to the Israelites, 'Come here and listen to the
words of the Lord your God. This is how you will
know that the living God is among you and that he
will certainly drive out before you the Canaanites,
Hittites, Hivites, Perizzites, Girgashites, Amorites
and Jebusites. See, the ark of the covenant of the
Lord of all the earth will go into the Jordan ahead
of you. Now then, choose twelve men from the

tribes of Israel, one from each tribe. And as soon as the priests who carry the ark of the Lord—the Lord of all the earth—set foot in the Jordan, its waters flowing downstream will be cut off and stand up in a heap.' So when the people broke camp to cross the Jordan, the priests carrying the ark of the covenant went ahead of them. Now the Jordan is at flood stage all during harvest. **Yet as soon as the priests who carried the ark reached the Jordan and their feet touched the water's edge, the water from upstream stopped flowing.** It piled up in a heap a great distance away, at a town called Adam in the vicinity of Zarethan, while the water flowing down to the Sea of the Arabah (that is, the Dead Sea) was completely cut off. So the people crossed over opposite Jericho. The priests who carried the ark of the covenant of the Lord stopped in the middle of the Jordan and stood on dry ground, while all Israel passed by until the whole nation had completed the crossing on dry ground. (Joshua 3:1-17 NIV, emphasis mine)

Did you catch that? The water did not stop flowing upstream until the priest's feet touched the water. They didn't stand on the edge and try to figure out how to make it happen, they took the step. What's even more exciting is if you notice, the text says that the Jordan (verse 15) was at a flood stage at that point. It wasn't a tiny little river that they could cross easily on their own; it was a raging flood.

I don't know about you, but that is a serious step of faith. It is yet another reminder that God is and has been preparing you for the work you are doing. He will prepare you, equip you, and get you to where you are ready, but there will come a time when you need to take the step and then watch Him work.

Years ago, I attended a Catalyst conference and Charles Stanley was asked how he had sustained fifty years in ministry. His answer perfectly sums up taking the step so beautifully. He said, "Obey God and leave the consequences to Him."[22]

So, what is it that is keeping you from taking the step? We need you. This world needs more women like you to step into the leadership roles that God has uniquely and precisely prepared you in this season. There is absolutely no one like you. I can say that with 100% authority. Even if you are a twin and you "look" identical chances are that your personalities are slightly different.

What is the thing that you would do if money and time were not an issue? Go ahead, take a minute and really think about this for a bit. Is it a ministry you would start? A book you would write? A class you would teach? A non-profit to help single moms? An after-school program for at risk kids? The list is endless, but you are going to have a very specific dream or purpose that God has created you to fulfill.

The world has tried to tell us that there is already someone out there doing the thing that we want to do or that we don't possibly have all the answers and probably won't be able to make it happen. My question to you is this, why are you listening to the world? You serve the great and mighty King Jesus, and He has made you more than a conqueror and He has certainly created you for such a time as this. So, again I will ask you, why are you listening to the world around you?

When you lead in the way He has created you to be, you slowly start to release the grip that fear has had on you like Peter did when he walked on water. You simply have to keep your eyes on Jesus and take the step. I'm not saying taking the step won't be scary because it probably will. Doing something new and different can be hard, even when it is something we really want to do. But do it afraid. You heard me. Do it afraid. Can I let you in on a little secret that no one has ever told you, or chances are that you didn't believe? We are all afraid. Ask anyone who did something you want to do, and chances are they will tell you they were terrified when they started as well. Fear is a completely normal part of trying new things. Do it afraid.

However, let me be clear that I am not advocating for stepping out of God's will to do our own thing. Not at all. I am 100 percent talking about being a woman who is praying, spending time in God's Word, and seeking good godly counsel for what she believes God is calling her to do. All of this has to happen before you take the step. You would never blindly just walk out in front of traffic and pray that Jesus would protect you, would you? It's the same thing as being obedient and owning your leadership. It's a tandem process with Jesus leading and you following. You don't go before Him. You wait for His lead.

Did you notice the part in the story we read earlier from Joshua 3 where Joshua takes the step of obedience to what God was preparing them for? Let me refresh your memory for a minute. Joshua 3:3-4 it says, "giving orders to the people: *'When you see the ark of the covenant of the Lord your God, and the Levitical priests carrying it, you are to move out from your positions and follow it.* Then you will know which way to go, since you have never been this way before. But keep a distance of about two thousand cubits between you and the ark; do not go near it'" (NIV, emphasis mine).

Two things stand out to me about taking the step:

1. When you see Him move, you follow Him. (Verse 3— When you see the ark move, you are to follow it.)

2. Then you will know where to go because you have never gone here before.

I would also encourage you to take the time, money, and energy to invest in yourself. It is always a good time to learn, grow and develop yourself as you prepare to take the step He is leading you to take. Here's a little note about this: investing in yourself as you prepare to take the step will not just happen automatically. You will need to schedule it and make it a priority. Block off time on your calendar to get it done. This is where it's important to know who you are and how you operate as a person and as a leader, which is another reason tests, like StrengthsFinder, are so helpful.

Over the years, I've heard numerous leaders encourage people to work on their strengths, not their weaknesses. We grow up thinking we must work on our weaknesses, but it is your strengths that will set you apart. You can build teams and support around your weaknesses but develop your strengths.

Taking the first step is sometimes simply taking a class or signing up for a training. This has been pivotal in my leadership development over the years, and I truly believe that it can be for yours as well. Sign up for conferences, trainings, webinars, and things that are going to help you develop as a female leader. The great thing is that there are so many online right now which means you can literally pick the time, block your calendar, and make it happen.

Something that can help you take this step is to look at a whole calendar year to determine the best times to invest in these opportunities. Figure out what's coming up and what would make the biggest impact on your development as a female leader. Then map it out; don't just randomly pick events and training but be intentional and selective about what is going to help you prepare to take that step. Is there a writing class you could use that will help you prepare for your book? Is there a speaker's training course that will help you with your on-stage presence? Is there a business class that could help you set up your ministry or non-profit in a smart business way for success from the get-go? What does that look like for you?

Look around and ask others which courses, trainings, and events have made the biggest impact on their development as a leader. Remember, we are now well-networked women, so you have other women who can help you.

Next, you are going to want to take a look at the cost of these training and events. Do you have a budget line designated for personal growth for the year? If so, see which of your options fit within your budget. If any or all of these exceed your budget, then talk to your leadership about why these would be beneficial for your development to see if they can increase your budget. You have to make the ask. Don't assume they know you want to go, and don't let them assume you don't want to go. Neither of these assumptions are true, right, or good for the organization. So just ask. Write up a proposal and a plan for your leadership development over the year. Explain how and why these will not only benefit you, but the organization as well. I am a firm believer that you don't have something because you haven't asked for it.

Real Ministry Chick Experience

from Joanna la Fluer

I've never heard anyone say that they wish they'd been less brave in a situation. Our regrets often come from moments where we wanted more courage, not less. Courage to tell them how we really feel, bravery to try a new thing, fortitude to end something that's run its course. I haven't made any significant life decision without a good dose of bravery. Bravery has served me well as I've stepped into the big wide unknowns in my life. I was brave enough to end a relationship that had turned toxic after many years together. I needed to be brave when I chose to live abroad in France, where I knew no one and could barely speak the language. I needed courage to say "Yes" to Jesus when He asked me to leave a city and community, I loved to take on an enormous challenge of skill and character at a church back in my hometown. More recently, I needed bravery to go out on my own as I grew my own business without those safety nets of salaries, retirement funds, and health insurance.

It's important, though, that I don't give you the wrong impression. I'm not all bravery and fearlessness. Generally, I have wrestled with anxiety for as long as I can remember. I used to be sick and throw up every time I spoke publicly or got on an airplane. Although I've done a lot of both in my life, I was wracked with fear about it for decades. Anyone who's worked or travelled with me knows I used to be notorious for this. I carried those airplane sickness bags around with me for a while. It led me to lean on God and a good professional counselor to get more freedom and healing in my life.

In the midst of the fears of anxiety that come and go, I have also determined to never let it stop me from what I felt were the dreams and calling on my life. I may have anxiety, but it will not be the boss of me. I want bravery to win. Anxiety does not serve me well, and it doesn't add a single hour to my life. In fact, I'm quite sure I've lost some years of my life because of it. Year by year, I'm being healed and freed up to be a braver woman. I know I have never regretted one brave moment. God has used them all to make me the kind of person that walks more closely with Him and trusts Him more fully with my future. As Amanda Cook sings, "He makes me brave."[23] My friends, whatever is in front of you today, let bravery be the boss of you.

I'll be honest with you for a moment. It might sound simple enough to make the ask, but I know that might not be the case and it certainly wasn't for me for many years. I didn't have enough confidence in myself and my leadership to make the ask. I wasn't owning my leadership and because of that I missed out on many opportunities to learn and grow from some of the industry's best leaders. This was not a win for me or the organization that I worked for at the time. So, in order to own our leadership, we need to take the step, and maybe, just maybe, do it afraid.

The challenge is to not let yourself get all tangled up in stress and nerves when you are trying to get your nerve up to make the ask. Therefore, it is so important to know who you are and the gifts you bring to the table. You will probably need to be flexible, so hold these courses, trainings, webinars, and conferences with open hands and a pliable heart. At this point you are really invested in making it happen and it is easy to get disappointed if it is a "no", a "not right now", or even a "please explain more about this" response from your leadership.

The goal here is not to win only for yourself but for the organization. If you have prepared a proposal of how and why you would benefit from attending this event, then you can go back to the list and share without being emotional, but simply from an informational standpoint. I think it is important to list the event specifics in bullet point form so that they are easy for those making the decision to review, skim, and process.

You are going to want to list details such as:

» Dates

» Location

» Host

» Cost (Include ticket price to attend as well as the estimated cost for the flight, rental car, food, etc. if you must travel.)

» Personal Benefits

» Organizational Benefits

What happens if you ask, lay it all out there, and still get a no or a not right now? It's tough not to be discouraged at this point, that much is true, but please don't let that stop you. You might not be able to do the specific training, events, courses, etc. that you originally wanted to do, but determine whether there another way to do something similar.

Think out of the box for a minute. Is there a cheaper alternative? Can you find some training on YouTube, Instagram, or a podcast? Can you reach out to your network and see if they can share their notes or biggest takeaways from an event or training that they attended? I have found that most of the time people are more than willing to help, especially another leader who is looking to grow.

Don't let money stop you. There are always alternatives to getting that training done. It might not look how you thought it would, but you never know, it might be better. One of the things I love best about being in the ministry is that even though there is never enough of a budget, and you are always having to find creative ways to get things done with what you have, you, your leadership, and your creativity are constantly being stretched to new levels.

Real Ministry Chick Experience
from Danielle Strickland

Transformation. Better Together.

Sometimes I wonder what the real problem is. I know the presenting problem is often a constant and subtle feeling that I don't really belong, that I don't deserve things, that I shouldn't want things, or those consistent thoughts that I'm not worth it in general. The promotion, the applause, the recognition all end up haunting me and turning up the volume of the dissonance in the foundations of my life that resonate with one big booming question—is this a mistake?

Apparently, most women have this accompanying dialogue. A church I know started to transform the way they do ministry a few years ago. In order to empower everyone, specifically women, to lead, they discovered some research that helped them understand why it was so hard for them to get women to come to the leadership table.

This research also starts to make sense in light of this internal (and sometimes external) dialogue so many women struggle with in their own life. A female's self-confidence peaks at 9 years old. You read that right. According to the most recent research, girls at age 9 are as self-confident as they are ever going to be. The reason? Well, there are many. But consider what puberty itself does to every girl's sense of self, followed by the dynamics of high school, and then the harsh and present realities of a dominant culture that continues to objectify and harass women. I know it sounds intense—but it's true.

1 in 3 girls will be sexually abused in her lifetime according to the most recent stats. 1 in 3. The felt reality of those statistics mean that it's almost 'normal' for girls to feel disempowered. But that's only half the story.

When I first heard the journey of the church I mentioned above, I was a little conflicted. They say it was hard for them to get women to come to the leadership table. Is it possible that women don't want to lead? Maybe this confirms those ideas we've all heard—that women aren't meant to lead? It's so hard to understand the problem this church leadership team had when I've been a witness to so many incredibly gifted, capable, educated, and equipped women who want to lead and just can't seem to get a seat at the table.

How can there be so many women who are able and willing to lead and so few places for them to do so? How can there be so many male leaders who want women to lead and can't find them? Rather than dismiss one group as the problem, I think it's a deeper truth to understand disconnection itself as the problem. How have we become so disconnected from each other? There is something fundamentally broken at the heart of how women and men connect. And it's been like that for a very long time. Think back to the story of Adam and Eve in the Garden in Genesis 3. When humanity severed their connection to God the next thing that broke was their relationship with each other! That's a deep wound.

Much of our current culture's conversation around this very topic is rooted in fear. The #MeToo movement saw over 19 million women publicly express their story of harassment and abuse in a little over a month and it seemed hardly anyone was spared.

Leaders, business men, Hollywood tycoons, fathers, churches, husbands, non-profit champions, governments, systems, and structures—so many people implicated and the pain so overwhelming. What do we do?

The temptation is to allow fear to lead us. And that would be such a terrible mistake. Fear is a tyrannical oppressor who will seek to silence, separate, and pit us against each other. If we are motivated by fear, what we do or don't do will become a tool for even more oppression. But there is another option—a Divine one. It's how Paul, the apostle, describes the Good News of Jesus to the Corinthian church (a church that knew all about divisions and fear). He describes it as the "ministry of reconciliation" (see 2 Corinthians 5:11-21), and this is such good news for our current context.

There is a way women and men can heal the divide and work together to transform the future. It's the way of Jesus. And I don't mean some pie in the sky kind of 'fairy dust' solution. What I mean by the 'way of Jesus' is the hard and beautiful work of making wrong things right again. This is the work of forgiveness (letting go of past hurts), repentance (being sorry and willing to make things right again), and transformed relationships (doing things differently and together). When we become infused with the love of God, we start to see how Jesus is turning our wounds into healing, our past into learning, our future into hope, our relationships into collaboration, our diversity into celebration, and our differences into mutuality—making our reconciliation the best collaboration for transformation the world has yet to see. And the world is so desperately hungry for help on this one.

I've never been more hopeful at the possibility of a shared future because I know we are not people motivated by or stuck in fear. We are the children of God. We are the redeemed. We are the brave ones, who, with God's presence and invitation can confront our fears and transform our reality with perfect love. We receive that love through Jesus and then we become that love with Jesus so that we can love this world into the wild, beautiful, fruitful, peaceful place it was always created to be.

I pray that this hope of the Gospel silences the whispering voices in the backdrop of women's lives that keep insecurity a blanket they hold onto. I pray it releases men to genuine repentance that leaves no regrets. I pray that it unleashes the Church to be a light on a stand, a city on a hill for the world to witness the possibilities of hope in a cynical time. But most of all I pray it makes a way for our children to live a future God has always dreamed for them—a reconciled future of collaboration for a transformed world.[24]

Chick CHAT

Real, practical advice from women in ministry with some tips you can share with other female leaders to help them learn how to take their next step:

There is always a purpose to the process. What has your process been that has led you to your purpose, to your next step? Follow the process that you got you to where you are and trust Him who lead you through to this point. He will see you through. – Sonia

When God calls me to step up in leadership, my choice is always to obey. His way IS always the best and He will always get the glory. He crowns me with confidence and gives me the insane courage I need.
– Jennie

Just say YES to God even if it's outside your comfort zone! That's where amazing things happen!!! – DeAnn

God will knock on the door of opportunity, but he is a gentleman it is our job to answer. – Tara

You can be content while contending for more. Your current season is always preparation for the next.
– Winter

The most vital action of a ministry leader is obedience. We must rely less on our own creativity and listen for

His directions so that we can lead our people into new, fun adventures with confidence. It is His ministry after all! – Katie

I once walked with a client through a difficult leave which ended up a to be the best thing for her. I might encourage someone here who needs to hear that too—sometimes leading well means leaving well—and that does not mean you are giving up on God or the people you love. – Kristen

A wise woman once told me . . . there is so so much JOY to be found in obedience. – Debbie

In taking the next step, listen to the people around you who are reflecting what Jesus is already telling your heart. And listen to them even if the rollercoaster of cant's arrive. These are people who love you and are reminding you to listen to that still small voice of Jesus inside telling you to step forward. Everyone believes in you but you. Trust them. – Dianne

I would add that for every door you open, every opportunity seized, every stained-glass ceiling you shatter . . . be sure you wedge your high heel in the doorway to make sure it's wide open for the women coming after you. Don't just look forward, keep an eye on how you can develop and empower those coming behind—in all likelihood they will be able to go further than you because you made the pathway easier. That's a win. – Kyla

You're the only person that can fulfill YOUR Purpose God has called you to. – Erin

If I'm not confident in my next step, it's usually because I'm not prepared, or I don't know what my next step is/haven't heard from God on the subject yet. To feel confident, I plan time in my schedule to pray and learn from God what he wants me to say or how to obey. I also plan time in my schedule to prepare for that step of obedience. Hear what God wants. Prepare to do that thing He is asking. Then, so that thing as best you can. – Stephanie

Taking your next step is not putting yourself forward, it's putting God forward. Using your gifts glorifies God. – Cami

I would tell her that every woman has both an internal critic and an inner counselor. The internal critic always gets loud when we move in the direction of our purpose and calling. The internal critic means well because that voice just wants to keep us safe and to avoid risk. But we also have an inner counselor. That still small voice that's calling us forward. Turn down the critical voice holding you back and ask yourself. Which of my values will I be honoring by moving forward? And then take a step from the energy of that value. – Jeannette

QUICK *Tips*

Practical tips for you to take the step:

- ✓ Research and find an event, training, course, or conference that will help you develop the skills you need to take that step.

- ✓ Ask other leaders you respect and admire which events, training, courses and conferences have helped them the most over the years.

- ✓ Set aside some time to pray through the question, "What is the thing that you would do if money and time were not an issue?"

- ✓ What do you feel like God is asking you to take the step on?

    - ✓ Is it in faith, is it in obedience, is it something that scares you?

- ✓ Spend time studying Joshua 3 and ask the Lord to reveal to you what He is showing you specifically by that story.

- ✓ What is one thing, not the entire plan, but one thing that you could do today, even if you did it afraid, that would be taking the step in your life?

Chapter 9

YOU WERE MADE FOR MORE: WHERE DO YOU GO FROM HERE?

Here we are, almost at the end of our journey together and it is my hope that along the way you have picked up some tools that will help you as a female leader to find your community, own your leadership, and take the step. Friend, you truly are more than just . . .

The end of the journey is also where we will start to wrestle with a new level of doubt. Your mind might be filled with a thousand different "what if?" scenarios and I wish that I could say that you won't deal with that, but chances are you will. We have a hard time grappling with the fact that the God of the Universe doesn't need us but chooses to use us in His ministry here on earth. Whatever specific call He has on your life you are still very much human and at some point, or another you might let the fears and doubts take the lead in your life over your faith. Oh, not at all on purpose, after all, we are Jesus loving girls, leading, loving, and serving His people in a variety of different ways. But, in our humanness we can take our eyes off Jesus, much like Peter eventually did when he stepped out of the boat and became overcome with fear. Some of those fears will be very real and present in your life and ministry and many of those will be stuck in our mind.

Here's my challenge to you. Every time you start to doubt, every time you start to go down the spiral of "what if?", I want you to change it in your mind and even out loud if you need to (I certainly have done this a few times myself), to "even if." Changing one word completely flips the narrative. Here's a few examples:

» What if I fail?

  » Even if I fail, my God will still love me. (Jeremiah 31:3)

» What if I make a fool of myself?

  » Even if I do make a fool of myself God will still be crazy about me. Who am I trying to impress, God or man? (Galatians 1:10)

» What if we lose all our money and it doesn't work?

  » Even if I lose my money my God will supply every need. (Philippians 4:19)

» What if I get sick, hurt, or something bad happens?

  » Even if I get sick, hurt, or something bad happens my God will never leave me. (John 16:32-33)

I've had to literally walk myself through that series so many times and every time it helps. It doesn't take the problem away, but it does put it into proper perspective. Another thing I noticed by going through the What If/Even If exercise is that the "What if?" section is based completely on what I can do or accomplish on my own. "Even if" is based completely on what God can do or accomplish that I cannot.

What if? = what I can accomplish

Even if! = what God can do

There's a big difference in the thinking associated with those two statements and they have helped me release the stress, pressure, or anxiety of taking the step and moving forward. If the whole "what if?" spiral doesn't start, then chances are the "I'm not good enough" spiral might threaten to keep you from moving forward. Friend, you are more than enough, not because you are all that and a bag of chips, but because God made you and He made you with a specific purpose and ministry in mind. The enemy would like you to get stuck in the cycle of feeling less than because it will keep you from doing the work God has called you to do. Oh yes, I am still talking to you, a female leader in the ministry.

You are out there doing the work, but we have all gone through seasons where we doubt ourselves, doubt our leadership, doubt our gifts, skills, talents, you name it. We need to let that stuff go. Right now, pass Go, collect $200 and move forward. I have talked to so many strong talented female leaders in the Church and ministry over the years and almost every one of them had some secret doubts. The little thing that had at one point or another kept them from moving into all the abundance God had for them. I am not talking about prosperity gospel here, I am talking about the full, radiant, abundant life that God has called each and every one of us to be a part of each day.

The people we lead need to see us living the full life in front of them. Our families need to see it, our friends need to see it, and the world needs to see that you can love Jesus, be a strong leader, and still have fun. You can live a passionate purposeful and intentional life while still enjoying the journey He has called to and still be fully you. You are not less than because of your height, weight, hair color, skin color, or ethnicity. As a matter of fact, every one of those things makes you absolutely beautiful in the sight of God and because you are walking in the confidence that you may not be perfect, but you are perfectly loved.

If the people we serve in ministry could see that, can you just imagine how it would impact them and their walk with God? Think about it. If you and I struggle with the "what ifs?" and the "I'm not good enough" stuff, don't you think there are people around you that are dealing with the very same thing? You bet they are! They might not be talking about it, but they are watching you. Are you living out what you say you love? Are you leading authentically from the heart? Are you using your gifts, skills, and talents each day for the glory of God?

Will you fall short and make mistakes? Um . . . yep. We *all* do (all fall short of the glory of God). You are still 100 percent human, so there will always be room for improvement, but what if the people you lead see you lead with truth and authenticity. They need to see that. We need you, friend. We need you to be the leader He created you to be. You are perfectly uniquely you as you are, not pretending to be perfect, but working hard to be more like Christ each day. Our world needs believers who love Jesus and make mistakes, but don't cover them up; they own them, apologize for them, and work to make things and themselves better.

We need you.

Just as you are.

To lead, love, and equip those God brought into your sphere to lead.

You are not a mistake, you are not "not enough" you are right where God has you for this season. You are more than just . . . it's time for you to find your community, own your leadership and take the step!

I can't wait to see what God does when you do!

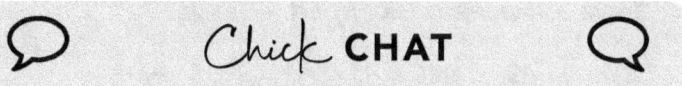

Chick **CHAT**

Real, practical advice from women in the ministry for those wrestling with the "what if's" and are trying to figure out if all the struggle of being a female leader in the church is worth it.

In answering my own question about whether it is worth it or not, I hold tight to, "Whatever you do, work at it with all your heart, as working for the Lord, not for human masters, since you know that you will receive an inheritance from the Lord as a reward. It is the Lord Christ you are serving." (Colossians 3:23-24 NIV) When people just don't show up, or what I do is never enough, or I'm left feeling unseen and unappreciated, I hold tight to doing what I do unto Christ. He always sees. He always knows. He always shows up. And He cares. – Sue

Do not confuse a challenging situation/circumstance/ environment with the authenticity of your calling. They can be 2 separate things. – Dianne

"What ifs" are not from your Father. He already knows. Don't listen to the enemy. – Danaka

Remember who you serve. God called you and placed you. We serve Him first. You serve His people and purpose as an extension of Him. The results are His responsibility. The obedience to serve as He leads is our part. – Jessica

If you impact ONE lady . . . it was all worth it!
– DeAnn

The idea of figuring out if it's "worth it" has always somewhat bothered me. Because whether or not something is "worth it" is completely personal. For me being a leader, specifically a leader in ministry, is worth it because it's truly the thing I've ever done where I can feel God uses every part of who I'm created to be. Other areas in my life use varying pieces of myself but in ministry I'm able to use all of my gifts and talents that God's given me, and I truly enjoy it. Because of that, what ifs don't scare me. They used to, for sure. I used to be scared. "What if they don't like what I say?" "What if I do this wrong?" "What if this goes so bad I lose all my people?" "What if this doesn't work and I can't pay my bills?" All those what ifs were rooted in fear of what others think and me trying to control things I can't. It's taken time and processing and I'm not always good at it all the time, but I had to let go of those things. Through this, it's allowed me to start leading out of my vulnerability and connect with more people and be truly amazed by God's provision. If you're leading where God is calling you and trusting that, the what ifs change from negative to positive. "What if God uses that dark story in my life to reach someone who's feeling lost and alone?" "What if I gain a new network of people for sharing these new ideas?" "What if I learn something new?" "What if God just provides and protects me?" – Bianca

"What if you and your ministry were literally the answer to someone's prayer? What if the gifts you bring to the table are just what that struggling soul needed to feel seen, heard and loved to truly experience the grace and mercy of Jesus? Being a woman in leadership is not always easy—but if we don't take up the challenge, we can miss the incredible blessings that come from serving others,

like being told how your words, your kindness, or your patience lifted someone out of a dark, lonely place. – Sonia

I never intended to be in full-time ministry, but God . . . My brother died in 2001 and I was a freshman in college. I had planned to be an education major and just couldn't sit in my classroom observations without crying. (Yeah. EMBARASSING!) So, I went to my advisor and told him I didn't want to leave school, but I couldn't do education at the moment. He encouraged me to take ministry/leadership classes. It was the best thing for my grief. I had professors who were walking through it with me and invested in my life and hurt. One would even email me almost daily to make sure I was eating, exercising and showering!! This is when I decided that I needed to be just like these leaders, ministers and loving people. If I could be for one other person what I needed in my lowest times, it would be worth it. Years later when dealing with post-partum anxiety and depression I was a lonely stay-at-home mom. It was such a struggle! Even then there were women who came in alongside of me and cared for me and my family! I had tonsillitis at one point and my husband was working. One such minister came to my home, loaded up two of my kids and took them to Chick-fil-A and the park. She was Jesus with chicken. I now look for the moms and dads who are struggling. The people I can best reach with my hands and feet.

Whenever another person is thinking about leaving the ministry, I will ask them if they are thinking of forever or just a season. If a season, I will encourage that they find a community of faithful friends to lean on in that time. If forever, I'll ask for their why. Not the why that makes them want to leave, but the why of their call in the first place. Has that changed or are you just tired? – Amanda

The Lord is not a God of "what ifs", He is the God of what is. He has called you, so rest in that truth because tomorrow will take care of itself. – Erin

QUICK *Tips*

Practical tips for you as you seek where to go from here:

✓ Write out a list of all the "what if's?" that are on your mind and keep you from taking the step.

  ✓ Go back through the list and right under it write out another line with an "Even if" statement, along with a Scripture to reference.

  ✓ Write a note to yourself on your mirror or in a place you will see it each day that says, "I am more than enough because _____". Fill in the blank with what God says.

  ✓ Write out a list of the people around you—not necessarily your friends—but those in your sphere that need to hear the message that they are enough as well.

  ✓ Who do you know that needs to read this book? Why don't you share a copy of it with them or take them to lunch and go through it together?

GROUP LEADER
Guide

Hey, Friend! Thank you for your willingness to go through this book with others. It's been my prayer that this book would be a resource for women in the ministry, whether you are brand new or have been serving in the church for many years.

On the next few pages, there are small group questions for you to use. These are for you to share with your group. They are intended to create community and allow the women in your group an opportunity to open up and be transparent with each other. By sharing our journey, the real journey, we can all be better than before and stronger female leaders in the ministry.

Here are a few tips when leading a group:

1. Make sure the women in your group feel welcome, seen, and heard. You can do this with a group within your ministry team, church staff, or even peer network. Wherever the women come from, do your best to make sure that each feels like she belongs there.

2. Provide a safe place for the women in your group. What is said or shared in your group needs to stay in your group. For women, especially women in the ministry, to feel safe and free to open up, they need to know that what they say will not show up in a prayer request or on social media.

3. Earnestly pray for the group before you meet, when you gather, and throughout the week. It doesn't have to be a long, detailed prayer

because God already knows what they are going through, but it should be a moment for you to keep them near your heart.

4. Try to minimize the distractions during your group time. You can do this by finding a space that is private and not out in the open where the women may not feel comfortable sharing.

5. Look for and include women that are going on the journey with you. This could lead to deep meaningful conversations and potentially even breakthrough moments in your leadership development and in building community with friends.

6. Encourage women to share, build connections with other women, and allow them time to process and think through their answers.

I would love to be a resource for you and your groups. Please contact me if there is any way I can support you as you walk with others through this content. Simply go to www.MelissaMashburn.com or email me at melissa@themashburnscg.com with your request.

Group Discussion Questions

Chapter 1 Group Discussion Questions:

1. What stood out to you in this chapter?
2. What challenged you?
3. Based on what you've read about your title and identity, in what ways do you struggle with the two being too tightly tied together?
4. Have you determined your core values?
5. What can you do today to establish your identity more firmly in Christ?
6. Who can you ask to walk alongside you as you work through your title and identity?

Chapter 2 Group Discussion Questions:

1. What was your biggest takeaway from this chapter?
2. What are your spiritual gifts?
3. What are some of your natural gifts? How do your natural gifts compliment your spiritual gifts?
4. What is one thing from the "practical solutions" section you can do starting this week?
5. Which is harder for you: knowing yourself, knowing your gifts, or investing in your leadership?
6. Who is someone you can ask to help you as you develop your leadership gifts and skills?

7. What is one class, webinar, training, or conference that you could grow from in this season? Now, what's holding you back from asking to attend it?

Chapter 3 Group Discussion Questions

1. What from this chapter connected with you?

2. What from this chapter challenged you?

3. Have you ever been the "only woman at the table" in your leadership?

4. Which of the tips listed is something you can apply starting today?

5. What tip would you add that might not have been listed?

6. Who is a woman that leads well that you could talk to about some of the things discussed in this chapter?

Chapter 4 Group Discussion Questions

1. What surprised you the most from this chapter?

2. What did you find to be an "aha!" moment in the chapter?

3. Which one of the tips could you use and apply to your ministry and life today?

4. What would you add that is not listed?

5. How can you connect with the other women in ministry at your organization?

6. Do you think it's possible that you've been "shrinking back" in your ministry or leadership?

GROUP DISCUSSION QUESTIONS

Chapter 5 Group Discussion Questions

1. If you are a mom who works in the ministry what has been your biggest struggle?

   a. What about your biggest blessing?

2. What is one practical tip from this chapter that you could put into practice this week in your ministry?

3. What can you do to help other moms in the ministry?

4. What does your church or ministry do to support moms?

   b. What about for your staff kids/families?

3. Who can you reach out to this week to offer a word of encouragement as they lead as a mom and in the ministry?

4. What would your ideal week look like as a mom and female leader?

   c. What's keeping that from being a reality in your ministry?

Chapter 6 Group Discussion Questions

1. Which of three areas of community do you struggle with the most?

   a. Community with God

   b. Community with family

   c. Community with friends

2. Why do you think that is currently true?

3. Do you have friends outside of the ministry?

4. How often do you network and connect with other women in the ministry outside of your organization?

5. What could you do this week to work on these connections?

6. Which of the tips from the Ministry Chick Facebook group stood out to you as something you should be aware of?

Chapter 7 Group Discussion Questions

1. When you hear the statement "Own your leadership", what does that mean to you?

2. What would you ask your leader for if you weren't worried about how they would respond to your request?

3. What is stopping you from making the request right now?

4. What classes or training have you done to develop your leadership?

5. Have you ever done a life plan? If so, what did you learn about yourself?

6. What has been the best investment you have made in your leadership development?

Chapter 8 Group Discussion Questions

1. Read Joshua 3 together as a group.

2. What stood out for you in the passage you just read?

3. What do you think your next step might be?

4. What's one thing you can do this week to start moving in that direction?

5. What conferences, events, or training would be beneficial to your leadership development?

6. How can we support each other towards taking the next step?

7. Which of the practical tips listed in this chapter is something you could do right now?

Chapter 9 Group Discussion Questions

1. How does the concept of "what if/even if" change your thinking?

2. What is keeping you from moving forward?

3. Who can you reach out to that will help hold you accountable to keep moving forward?

4. Answer the question out loud, "What's next?"

5. What are you going to do with the information you've learned while reading this book?

6. Write out a message to yourself on an index card and place it where you can see it every day.

Real Ministry Chick
Experience Contributors

Crystal Stine is the author of *Holy Hustle* and *Quieting the Shout of Should*, speaks to groups around the country, and serves as the Communications and Online Director for her church. You can connect with her online at www.crystalstine.me, on Instagram @crystalstine, or join more than 175,000 people who have completed her free YouVersion devotionals! Crystal lives in Pennsylvania with her husband Matt and their daughter Madison.

Jessie Cruickshank is Founder of WHO-ology, ordained minister, neuro-ecclesiologist, and Director of Certification at The Future Church Company.

Cathie Ostapchuk is Co-Founder and Lead Catalyst of Gather, a national movement which exists as a catalyst to connect, equip, and mobilize women in Canada for leadership influence. She is a published author of *Brave Women, Bold Moves*, Choosing Courage in a Culture of Conformity, and was awarded the Best Christian Living book award from The Word Guild. Cathie co-hosts the HerInfluence Podcast and is a national speaker for www.LeaderImpact.ca. Cathie is focused on developing the leaders of today and tomorrow.

Kristin Fry is the author of "Beyond the Swipe", Speaker, Consultant at www.kristinfry.com.

Rev. Dr. Candace M. Lewis is the President and Dean of Gammon Theological Seminary at the Interdenominational Theological Center in Atlanta, Georgia. She is the first woman to serve in this role in the school's 138-year history. Candace is an ordained Elder in the United Methodist Church and previously served as a District Superintendent of the Gulf Central area of the Florida Annual Conference. Her first book was published January 2019, *Resurgence: Navigating the Changing Ministry Landscape,* and is available for purchase on Amazon.

Frances Chaisson is married to husband Jeff. They share the work of ministry together at Salty Church where they both manage the operations of Salty Family Services, a social services ministry dedicated to strengthening families and keeping children out of foster care. Frances is also a Master Certified Wellness Coach at www.franceschaisson.com.

Jessica Bealer is the author of *"Don't Quit: The Best Things In Ministry Come Over Time"*, Speaker, Consultant www.generis.com/jessica-bealer.

Jaclyn Weidner is the host of *Ready to Thrive,* an equipping and encouraging you to move from surviving to thriving podcast. You can find her podcast at www.jaclynweidner.com/podcast.

Toni Nieuwhof is an author of *Before You Split: Find What You Really Want for the Future of Your Marriage,* speaker, and family law mediator, and has spent decades of her professional life practicing law and combining her professional careers of pharmacist and lawyer in leadership roles for hospitals. www.toninieuwhof.com.

Carrie Ann Williams is the CEO of Leadership Network, Founder and CEO of The Truth Republic and is passionate about women discovering, developing, and deploying into their unique God given calling. Carrie has over 20 years of full-time ministry experience. She has held leadership positions in global mission organizations, nonprofits, and churches, including being part of the core leadership team that launched The Church of Eleven22. She feels most alive when she is preaching, writing, spending quality time with the people she loves and being a crazy creative person. www.thetruthrepublic.com.

Angie Ward is a leadership author and teacher with over 30 years of ministry experience in church, parachurch, and educational settings. She is the author of *I Am a Leader: When Women Discover the Joy of Their Calling* and general editor of the Kingdom Conversations book series. She currently serves as Assistant Director of the Doctor of Ministry program at Denver Seminary.

Joanna la Fluer is the Executive Director of Word Made Digital, speaker, podcaster, TV host, and communications consultant at www.joannalafleur.com.

Danielle Strickland is the author of *Better Together: How Women and Men Can Heal the Divide and Work Together to Transform the Future.* She is a Spiritual Leader, Justice Advocate, Communicator, and Peacemaker, you can find more information about Danielle at www.daniellestrickland.com.

Chick Chat *Contributors*

Amanda	Danaka	Jen	Marlena	Sabrina
Amy	Dawn	Jennie	Meredith	Samantha
Angela	DeAnn	Jerra	Michelle	Sara
April	Debbie	Jessica	Natalie	Shakema
Aria	DeDe	Julie	Noreen	Shari
Becky	Dianne	Kathy	Pamm	Sonia
Bekah	Erin	Katie	Penny	Stephanie
Bianca	Gena	Katylin	Pip	Sue
Brenda	Gina	Kelly	Rachael	Susan
Cami	Heather	Kim	Rebekah	Tara
Carol	Jaimme	Kristen	Rehana	Tiffany
Christie	Janie	Kyla	Rosemarie	Winter
Crystal	Jeannette	Lori	Roslyn	Yvonne

Acknowledgments

If there is one thing that I have learned over the years, it is that no one gets anything done by themselves. Yes, there are certainly times and seasons where we work alone and we are supposed to do the thing that God has called us to, but to be honest, the majority of my life, ministry and work has been done with and through other amazing people.

My husband Matt is my Number One cheerleader, my support, and my rock. He has encouraged me to chase the dreams that God has laid on my heart and cheered me up when I felt weighed down by the burden of the call or my own self-imposed limitations. He has been my constant source of, well, everything for over twenty-eight years, and I can honestly say that it just keeps getting better. Thank you, my love, for believing in me even when I doubted myself. I am truly better because of you.

Right outside of my amazing husband is our incredible family. Our sons, Nick and Bailey, and their beautiful brides, Ashley and Jules, have made our family better and more beautiful. Thank you for being a source of my greatest joy and my greatest learning experiences over the years. I would also be remiss if I didn't mention my mom, dad, and sister. They have, even from my childhood, believed the best in me . . . always. They taught me that I could be anything, do anything, and accomplish anything that I put my mind to. Because of you I am the woman that I am today, and I am deeply grateful to be called your daughter and sister. I've also been incredibly blessed with amazing in-laws, which we call "in-loves" in our family. I jokingly say that my mother-in-love might actually be my biggest cheerleader. You are certainly the biggest catalyst of my spiritual growth, and for that, there are simply no words.

Over the course of my life and ministry, there have been so many amazing women that I have been blessed to serve alongside, lead, coach, teach, and simply get in the trenches with. I watched them lead well while learning more about myself in the process. They are pioneers in so many ways, and I could not be where I am without going on the journey, be it a few months or a few years, with these women. This also includes my counselors and those who have walked this journey with me over my ministry career and helped me process and be a healthier leader. Thank you for being women I can learn from and grow with.

My girlfriends in the "Best Small Group Ever" as well as the women who have journeyed through many of life's storms over the years (Michelle, Laura, Nancy, Mercy, Noreen, and so many more). Thank you for listening to my big ideas, for believing in me, and for letting me talk your ears off after a women's event or Bible study. I love you all dearly.

My mentor, coach, cheerleader, and most importantly friend, Kadi Cole. You challenged me, pushed me to lead well and grow exponentially more where God has uniquely gifted me. Your Marco Polo messages made me laugh, inspired me, and always came at just the right time. Thank you for allowing me the privilege to walk alongside you in this ministry called Ministry Chick and for believing in bigger things for me than I could have ever imagined. You truly champion women and I've been blessed because of it.

There isn't a book, blog, event that can come together completely on its own; it is built and developed and made even better by those who use their expertise and experience to clear away the chaff from the wheat. This book has been loved on and developed by Charlotte Allison, Carolyn Reed Master, our Creative team girls (Karina, Kierra, Tiana, and Kristina), Mandy Roberson, and the team over at Market Refined Media (with Danielle and Nelly for coming through in crunch time). Thank you for your prayers, encouragement, support, kick in the tail when needed, and expertise. This book would not be done to the level that it is without each of you, so thank you!

To the women in the private Facebook community called Ministry Chick. You are who I wrote this book for. You have inspired me with your transparency, authenticity, and your willingness to grow as female leaders in the church. Thank you for your faithfulness in serving wherever God has placed you and for your willingness to walk alongside each other throughout it. Your stories, practical tips, and ideas are what makes this book *for* you and also *by* you.

None of this would even be remotely possible without Jesus. He saved me, redeemed me and made me new. I have walked many miles in the trenches doing the work of the ministry and over the last two decades my love for Him has grown even deeper because He took my mess and made something marvelous out of it. Thank you, Father, for pursuing me. I will make it my life's work to make Your name known. To Him be the glory, amen.

About Ministry Chick,
the Facebook Community

Opening Doors for Female Leaders

A community of like-minded individuals serving in the trenches of ministry together.

This is our **safe place**.

A place to be **understood**.

A place to **belong**.

A place to **learn**.

A place to **THRIVE**.

Ministry Chick is a community dedicated to helping women work through what it means to be an effective female leader in ministry.

We invite our members to post questions, prayer requests, resources, and experiences as a means to building community and supporting each other as we navigate life and ministry as female leaders.

If you have any questions, please feel free to contact Melissa Mashburn, Executive Director for Ministry Chick at melissa@themashburnscg.com.

For more information about how we can serve you and your church, please visit melissamashburn.com or kadicole.com.

Ministry Chick was created as an extension of Kadi Cole & Company and is now run and led by Melissa Mashburn of The Mashburns Consulting Group in partnership with Kadi Cole & Company.

About the *Author*

Melissa has invested more than 20+ years serving the local church on various staff teams ranging in size from 90 to over 40,000 in weekend attendance. She currently serves at Southeast Christian Church which ministers to over 40,000 people weekly. Melissa has had various roles, including executive level leadership and an extensive background in communications, marketing, membership, groups, first impressions, weekend service development, children's ministry, and women's ministry.

Melissa runs the private Facebook group Ministry Chick (originally founded by Kadi Cole & Company) where she leads more than 3300 women from all over the world. In the Ministry Chick group, she hosts webinars, builds community, and provides the resources and connections for female leaders in the church.

Her specialty is working with women in ministry—at the local church, in nonprofits, and in personal ministries. She coaches female leaders to transform their thinking and renew their gifts, skills, and leadership. She offers individual coaching to women in ministry as well as consulting with churches and female leaders.

She and her husband, Matt, co-founded a company called The Mashburn's Consulting Group, where they offer practical solutions for growth for churches and non-profits, but the training, insight, and information can be transferred to businesses as well. They love to work alongside churches, ministries, and leaders who want to grow either in attendance, giving, leadership abilities, volunteers, or finances, etc.

As a connector, she loves to put the people that God puts in her path together. She believes the connections we have are not just for our good but for the good of others, and when you place people together who can encourage, strengthen, and build each other up in ministry or business then everyone wins.

Matt has been her best friend for over 29 years, and they have two adult sons, Nick, and Bailey, and two beautiful daughters-in-love, Ashley (married to Nick), and Jules (married to Bailey) You can find out more and get connected with Melissa at www.MelissaMashburn.com.

Endnotes

1   Lee Colon, "A Lesson from Roy A. Disney on Making Value-based Decisions," *Inc.*, July 24, 2019, https://www.inc.com/lee-colan/a-lesson-from-roy-a-disney-on-making-values-based-decisions.html.

2   Karla Pope, "50 Quotes From Women That Are All About Strength and Empowerment," *Good Housekeeping*, March 7, 2022, https://www.goodhousekeeping.com/life/g38335193/strong-women-quotes/.

3   Michael Hyatt, "No, You Don't Have to be Great at Everything – And Why You Shouldn't Even Try," Full Focus (blog), June 22, 2015, https://fullfocus.co/great-at-everything/.

4   Simon Sinek, "We can't be good at everything. If we were, there would be no need for teams," LinkedIn, April 2022, https://www.linkedin.com/in/simonsinek/recent-activity/.

5   Darrell W. Johnson, *The Glory of Preaching: Participating in God's Transformation of the World* (Westmont: InterVarsity Press, 2010) 182, https://www.google.com/books/edition/The_Glory_of_Preaching/Qa6TeHBzWHEC?hl=en&gbpv=0.

6   Maria Pellicano, *The Art of Powerful Communication* (Lulu.com, 2016), Chap. 13, https://www.google.com/books/edition/The_Art_of_Powerful_Communication/gf9iEAAAQBAJ?hl=en&gbpv=0.

7   Andrew Esparza, "How the Church Can Combat the Rise of Depression and Loneliness," ACTechnologies (blog), December 2, 2021, https://www.acstechnologies.com/church-growth/how-the-church-can-combat-the-rise-of-depression-and-loneliness/.

8   Cigna, "Cigna 2018 U.S. Loneliness Index," 2018 Loneliness Survey Findings Fact Sheet (pdf), https://www.cigna.com/static/www-cigna-com/docs/about-us/newsroom/studies-and-reports/combatting-loneliness/loneliness-survey-2018-updated-fact-sheet.pdf.

9   Ibid.

10 Barna, "How Mental Health is the New Domain of Ministry to the Next Generation," October 8, 2020, https://www.barna.com/research/mental-health-next-gen/.

11 Samantha DiFeliciantonio, "The Power of Communication: Helen Keller," TeamBonding (blog), February 10, 2014, https://www.teambonding.com/power-of-communication/.

12 Aimee Groth, "You're the Average of the Five People You Spend the Most Time With," Business Insider (blog), July 24, 2012, https://www.businessinsider.com/jim-rohn-youre-the-average-of-the-five-people-you-spend-the-most-time-with-2012-7#:~:text=David%20P%20Brown%20Motivational%20speaker,the%20average%20of%20all%20outcomes.

13 BSM Media Group, "A Conversation with Dr. Maya Angelou," *BSM Magazine* (audio interview), July 4, 2012, https://bsmandmedia.com/a-conversation-with-dr-maya-angelou/.

14 Jasmine Barta, "13 Dr. Suess Quotes to Live By," *USA Today*, July 11, 2013, https://www.usatoday.com/story/college/2013/07/11/13-dr-seuss-quotes-to-live-by/37436615/.

15 http://rightnowmedia.org

16 Craig Groeschel, "GLS18 Session Notes – Craig Groeschel – Becoming a Leader People Love to Follow," August 16, 2018, https://globalleadership.org/articles/leading-others/gls18-session-notes-craig-groeschel-becoming-a-leader-people-love-to-follow/.

17 C. Screechinth, *Powerful Quotes of Winston Churchill* (Mass Market Paperback, 2016) 9, https://books.google.com/books?id=fEgCEAAAQBAJ&pg=PA9&lpg=PA9&dq=what+-book+did+the+quote+"Mountaintops+inspire+leaders,+but+valleys+mature+them."+—+Winston+Churchill&source=bl&ots=H_KJTWPdOM&sig=ACfU3U3Y4MNnuO7BAJ26M2lxNqvB6zL3o-A&hl=en&sa=X&ved=2ahUKEwi06_K8zJ73AhVOjYkEHUwJB_4Q6A-F6BAgUEAM#v=onepage&q&f=false.

18 Stan Toler, *The Power of Your Attitude: 7 Choices for a Happy and Healthy Life* (Eugene: Harvest House, 2016) 67, https://www.google.com/books/edition/The_Power_of_Your_Attitude/ZBAVDQAAQBAJ?hl=en&gbpv=0.

19 Susan Vandenheuvel, "Created for Impact with Melissa Mashburn," February 16, 2021, *She Connects* (podcast), mp3 audio, https://sheconnects.podbean.com/e/created-for-impact-with-melissa-mashburn/.

20 I (Angie) put "guy things" in quotation marks to indicate that these were cultural stereotypes, not because I am implying that any type of interest is acceptable or unacceptable based on gender.

21 I (Angie) wrote a book with this very title—*I Am a Leader: When Women Discover the Joy of Their Calling*—in which I tell more of my own story and explore the unique journey and challenges of women ministry leaders.

22 I paraphrased this statement from hearing Charles Stanley say it at a Catalyst conference in 2019 in Atlanta, GA when he was asked how he sustained fifty years in the ministry.

23 Amanda Lindsey Cook (author and vocalist), "You Make Me Brave (Live)," recorded at the Civic in 2013, track 1 on *You Make Me Brave* by Bethel Music, https://bethelmusic.com/chords-and-lyrics/you-make-me-brave-you-make-me-brave/.

24 Used with permission by the author, Danielle Strickland. https://churchsource.com/blogs/ministry-resources/transformation-better-together.

www.ingramcontent.com/pod-product-compliance
Lightning Source LLC
Chambersburg PA
CBHW071152130626
46553CB00004B/1623